Daughters of Fire

Igniting Your Passion For God
In An Increasingly Dark World

Dear Reni,
Thank you so much
for the support.
Let it BURN!

Chris

CHRISTINA PATTERSON

ISBN-13: 978-1537158266
ISBN-10: 1537158260

Dedication

To Grandma Ruby. Your laughter and zeal to celebrate life will always brighten my soul.

Acknowledgments

Heavenly Father. You are my everything. Thank You for always seeing my potential over my past and present. Your love and faithfulness are always near. I love you forever.

Donald. You are my love. The longer we are united the more I realize how blessed I am to be your wife. You give me joy, strength and much laughter. I love you always.

Victoria. You are my firecracker. You brighten every day that I'm with you. Never let anything takeaway your fire for life. And remember, your mama always loves you.

Donald III. You are my warrior. You have given me courage I never knew I had. Always fight for what is true and just. And remember, your mama always loves you.

Mom. Your love is endless and it forever fuels my soul. I love you.

Dad. Your encouragement inspires me to go further and burn brighter. I love you.

Shadé. Thank you for your continued support and gentle spirit. Love you sis.

Quina. This book was a labor of love that would not have been birthed without your brilliant editing. I am so grateful you came alongside me on this journey. Love you sis.

Contents

The light shines in the darkness, and the darkness has not overcome it. — John 1:5

Introduction

There's never been a better time than now for the daughters of God to allow their passion for God to burst into flames, flames that will bring much needed light into this dark world. I believe this because light shines brightest in the dark. However, we must understand that the light we speak of only comes from a burning passion to live for God.

I'm thinking that's why you're ready to turn the pages of this book. You want that passion. You want the fire. I completely understand. I do too. This desire of ours raises some questions, like how can we be light in a world that would much rather see our fire for God extinguished? How can we continue to follow Jesus in a world that is quickly turning from Him? How can we visibly express our passion for God when we are constantly faced with temptation and sin?

If there is anyone best equipped to answer these questions it is the prophet Elijah. He steps into Israelite history at a time when God's people are suffering from the greatest spiritual gap between themselves and God. Still, Elijah is on a mission to not only continue in his own spiritual faithfulness, but to also turn the hearts of the Israelites back to God. He does so in the presence of widespread idol worship, immoral leadership, and temptation to give up all around. Sound familiar? Despite the dark and seemingly impossible circumstances, Elijah continues to stand boldly for God, surrender to God's will, and complete his mission.

That being said, I invite you to take a journey with me to learn from Elijah how we can actually burn bright for God in an increasingly dark world. We'll pull out biblical wisdom and practical life lessons from the life of Elijah that will encourage and empower us to live a passionate life for Christ.

Now, I know you may very well already have an all-consuming desire and passion for God. You've seen and tasted how good God is, which is why you desire more of Him. Our journey with Elijah will then serve to remind you how worthy our God is and encourage you to stay the course.

On the other hand, maybe this book finds you in the pits of sin and the furthest from God you have ever been. But there is this deep-down spark for God on the inside that you're afraid to pursue because you're scared of what that means you'll have to let go of. This book is for you too.

Or maybe you have been living for Christ for a long time, completely faithful to Him day in and day out. But now your walk with Christ is feeling mundane and dare I even say . . . boring. Let me tell you, this book is the fuel that you need for your fire.

I do need to note, however, that this book is not written so that we can feel good about ourselves by checking off "Be a good Christian girl" from our bucket list. As we'll learn, living a passionate life for Christ goes far beyond ourselves.

Regardless of how dim or bright your fire for God is, this book will take your passion for God to the next level. So will you join Elijah and me on this journey? We'll tear down some idols and face some fears, but we'll ultimately end up wiser, stronger, and burning bright.

Ready? Good. Let's go.

CHAPTER ONE

Stars: Shining Bright in the Dark

Now Elijah the Tishbite, from Tishbe in Gilead, said to Ahab,
"As the LORD, the God of Israel, lives, whom I serve, there will be
neither dew nor rain in the next few years except at my word."
— 1 Kings 17:1

I had no choice but to look up in awe and give praise to the Maker of our universe. A spring break trip to Guatemala took me to a rural village called Mam in the city of Xela. The host family we stayed with was kind and beyond generous. They were so patient with my limited Spanish, and we shared laughs about my lumpy attempt at making tortillas. Their home had enough electricity for a few lights and one TV, but they had no floors. The bathroom was a hole in the ground a few feet from the house.

On the night I stayed there, my classmate and I decided to use the bathroom before going to sleep. As we started to walk back to our room, I happened to look to the left. I saw the mountain range we traveled to visit our host family earlier that day, and right above that I witnessed a sight that took my breath away and left me only to worship the God of the cosmos.

Right before my eyes were thousands upon thousands of stars. I saw more stars from that one glance than I had ever seen collectively in my entire life. If I go to my own backyard right now in North Carolina I can probably count the stars on one hand. However, all those thousands upon thousands of stars I saw in Guatemala are still in the sky here in North Carolina as well. I just can't see them. This is because of an occurrence that scientists call light pollution. This happens when a lot of artificial light from highly populated areas greatly reduces the visibility of stars.

If the daughters of God were compared to stars, I would say we have some light pollution. There are many women who have placed their faith in Christ, but not as many showing visible signs of such a commitment. Plainly put, we are not allowing our light to shine. Our passion and fire for God has been snuffed out by the pollution of sin, idols, legalism, and anything that keeps us from sincerely connecting with our Maker.

We might attribute this to the dark times we live in, and if you've watched the news lately you know that we are in some dark times. We think that darkness snuffs out light, but it doesn't. Quite the opposite. The darker the atmosphere, the brighter the stars, just as I experienced in Guatemala. So now is the time for God's daughters to shine brightest. And we shine for God when we burn for Him with a consuming passion to live for Him.

If there is anyone who can help us to develop this passion for God, even in the midst of such darkness, it's the prophet Elijah. If we are stars, he is a shooting star. I have never seen a shooting star other than in a movie, so I can only imagine the wonder and awe I would feel if I were to see one in real life—shooting across the sky, lighting up the night, coming from Heaven straight to Earth as if out of nowhere. I believe a shooting star is a good comparison to the entrance of Elijah in the Bible. His first appearance seems to come out of nowhere, and he could not have come at a better time. Elijah is first introduced in 1 Kings 17, and the first two words of his introduction are packed with meaning: "Now Elijah . . . ." To understand the significance of this introduction we

need to understand what brings us to the "now" that
Elijah faces.

NOW

Elijah appears in Israelite history after a long string
of kings known for their evil ways. For the Israelites,
history repeated itself with one evil king after another.
There was Jeroboam, and then after him was Baasha.
After Baasha was Elah. After Elah was Zimri. After Zimri
was Omri. The only thing that seems to change from one
king to the next is the name. This lineage of kings was
filled with evil, murder, greed, idol worship, and sin so
great they exponentially aroused the anger of God. Not
one king had come to power in the Northern Kingdom,
where Elijah enters, who did what was right in the eyes of
the Lord. As a matter of fact, each king did more evil than
the king before him. And just when you think matters
couldn't get any worse, a man named Ahab becomes the
king. He was the most evil king in Israelite history. These
are not my words. The Bible goes into great detail as to
how Ahab was so evil.

Like the other kings before him, Ahab committed
the sins of worshiping idols and turning the hearts of the
Israelites away from God. But this was mere child's play to

Ahab. No big deal. Ahab also marries Jezebel who was a
Sidonian, the very people God warned the Israelites not to
intermarry with lest their hearts be turned from God to
worship other gods. (Deuteronomy 7:1-3) And that is
exactly what happened next. Ahab began to serve and
worship Baal, the false god of his wife. Ahab set up altars
to Baal and idols for the Israelites to worship. Had you
lived under the rule of Ahab at this time, it would have
been very difficult to avoid the worship of Baal because of
his significant political and social popularity. For all these
reasons the Bible tells us Ahab not only did more evil in
the eyes of the Lord, but also did more to arouse the anger
of the Lord than any king before him. And if we look back
at the history of Israelite kings up until this point, that had
to be pretty bad. He was the best of the worst.

This history of growing evil among the Israelites
bring us to 1 Kings 17 verse one, word one: "now."

> *Now Elijah the Tishbite, from Tishbe in Gilead, said to
> Ahab, "As the LORD, the God of Israel, lives, whom I
> serve, there will be neither dew nor rain in the next few years
> except at my word." – 1 Kings 17:1*

This "now" was the atmosphere in which Elijah is
introduced: an atmosphere filled with sin, a government

that endorsed the worship of false gods, and corruption. The Israelites' hearts were turned from their God, and their distance from Him was at its greatest. Despite this dark atmosphere, Elijah boldly steps to the evil King Ahab. This encounter between Elijah and Ahab is extremely brief; however, there is so much to learn from Elijah in this one verse about what it means to be a Daughter of Fire. Elijah's light was desperately needed during this dark time of Ahab's rule. In the same way, our light is needed now more than ever before. **I want to outline three key characteristics that made Elijah's light shine so bright.**

UNASHAMED

Usually when we meet someone for the first time we try to find something in common with that person, whether it is where they live, if they have children, or what they do for a living. And if all else fails we just start talking about the weather. We want to alleviate the awkwardness of first encounters by making a common connection with that person. Well, someone didn't tell this to Elijah because before he even tells Ahab his name he makes it known that he is a servant of the God of Israel. He begins his introduction to Ahab with the very thing that they do not have in common.

Elijah was letting Ahab know that Elijah was not here on his own behalf, but that everything he said and did should be accredited to the God of Israel. This was important then, and it is still important today. We live in a generation where we are tempted to give credit to every person and everything but God. But, the most important thing people need to know about us is that we serve the Lord. As great as we may be, none of us has never laid down our own life to save the souls of all mankind. **So more than people need to know us, they need to know Jesus.** And as happy and bright and loving as we may be, no one will know where our light comes from unless we tell them. Like Elijah, we live in a "now" situation where there are many gods that people worship and idols that people serve. So in order to be effective in bringing His light into a dark world, we cannot be ashamed to let people know Who we serve.

How much boldness Elijah must have had to step to the king who worshipped Baal and married Jezebel, and let him know, "I serve God." If I can be honest with you, sometimes I get nervous about telling someone I just met that I'm a Christian, or to say the name Jesus. People can get so offended these days, but Elijah reminds me of how important it is to not be ashamed. Offended or not, Jesus is the only God I know out there saving people from their sins and enabling them to know the One True God of Israel. He is the only God who rose from the dead and grants that same power to all who place their faith in Him. This is nothing to be ashamed of. We are reminded:

> *For I am not ashamed of the gospel, because it is the power of God that brings salvation to everyone who believes: first to the Jew, then to the Gentile. – Romans 1:16*

What makes Elijah such a powerful and legendary prophet is his boldness despite his "now" situation. Although times were at their worst, he did not use that as an excuse to cower, hide, or try to blend in. **In the same way, God is not calling us to hide from the darkness, but to be the light that this dark world desperately needs.** Jesus reminds us:

> GOD IS NOT CALLING US TO HIDE FROM THE DARKNESS. HE IS CALLING US TO BE THE LIGHT

> *"You are the light of the world. A town built on a hill cannot be hidden. Neither do people light a lamp and put it under a bowl. Instead they put it on its stand, and it gives light to everyone in the house. In the same way, let your light*

shine before others, that they may see your good deeds and glorify your Father in heaven." – Matthew 5:14-16

Our standing out is the very thing that will glorify our God as our light is a reflection of the God we serve. So the first thing we can do to let our light shine is to open our mouths and unapologetically proclaim that we are servants of the Most High God.

HUMBLE

As I mentioned, Elijah introduces his God before he even introduces himself. You see, God is about to do something big. He is about to show the Israelites His true power and remind them why He is the One True Living God deserving of their monogamous affection and worship. Although Elijah is the one prophesying about this drought, and it will not end until he says so, it is only by the power of God that this will happen. Elijah was bold to let his light shine unashamedly, yet he was humble in letting Ahab know he was simply a reflection of God's glory. We might not think that someone who is bold can also be humble. But I propose to you that Elijah was both. In fact, it was his humility that enabled him to be so bold.

Elijah was called to one of the most challenging

missions. God was going to use Elijah to turn the hearts of the Israelites back to Himself. Nothing like this had been done before in this generation. It was a task Elijah could not have done in his own might. He would need God's power and not his own to accomplish this mission. This is why Elijah's humility was so important. If he did not understand that turning this "now" situation around would only be done in God's power, then he would have lost some of his boldness. All the responsibility would be on him, and that is too much for one person to handle. So by humbling himself he was able to realize it was not up to him, but it was up to God to make it happen. Humility is a key component to being bold for God in the first place. If we want to be bold and unashamed for God, we must humble ourselves before Him. And by *humble* I do not mean shy or timid. That is not humility. The Bible tells us that "humility is the fear of the Lord; its wages are riches and honor and life." (Proverbs 22:4)

"Fear" in this verse means respect (to give proper honor) or reverence (to hold in high regard). **The Bible is telling us that humility is not putting ourselves down, it's lifting God up.** Like Elijah, it's allowing our lives to be used as a vessel to

> HUMILITY IS NOT PUTTING OURSELVES DOWN, IT'S LIFTING GOD UP

reflect God's glory that through us the world may know Him. It's a life that says Christ is greater, Christ is enough, Christ is all. Humility is not shying away. It's placing our life on display for God's glory alone by giving honor and glory where it is due.

Maybe God has called you to a very challenging and seemingly impossible task, one that has never been done before. Maybe you are the first to go to college in your family. Maybe you are the first to have children among your siblings and friends. Maybe you're recently married but you come from a family line of divorce. Many times God will call us to things that we have not seen done successfully, and we have no blueprint to follow or shoes to fill. Be that as it may, when we approach the mission God has granted us with humility we realize completing this mission is not up to us. It's up to God.

Elijah was called to break a pattern that no king before was able to overcome. The other kings failed because they did not rely on God. They were powerful and had endless resources at their hands, but they did not have the strength to do what God called them to do. Yet here we have Elijah from some town we know little about that is doing something no king has been able to do.[1] Why? **Because he humbled himself before God.** This is an excellent reminder that just because things have historically been one way does not mean they have to stay in a pattern of sin and brokenness. God is calling us higher.

Sometimes we can look at our "now" situation and be tempted to think, *Well this is how things have always been, so this is how things will always be.* When we think like this we make our history our god. But when we humble ourselves we realize our past is not greater than our God. It is then that we stop limiting God to only what has been done in the past. It is then that we will start seeing healing, restoration, peace, and reconciliation where it has never been seen before. Maybe you have been in the same destructive pattern of sin all your life. Maybe you come from a long family history of drug use, alcoholism, fatherlessness, or physical and/or sexual abuse. I want to let you know that your past does not dictate what God can do or will do in your life.

Spiritually the Israelites had been dry, and now God was going to bring a severe drought to the land and make their flesh as empty and dry as their souls. God may not have had their devout worship yet, but He would soon have their attention. God was ready to do a new thing to their souls, one they had been lacking due to worthless idol worship and now due to the worship of the false god Baal. God wanted to restore their souls in a way that had not been experienced by Israel collectively in generations. God wants the same for us. He wants to take the impossible in our world and our lives, and turn it around for His glory. And He will when we humble ourselves before Him.

NIGHT VISION

Did you know there is light all around us that we do not have the capacity to see with the naked eye? Scientists, however, have created all types of sensors and devices that enable us to see far beyond our physical capacity. For example, night vision technology collects all light in an area, even light we cannot see, and amplifies it so we may see clearly in the dark.[2] The baby monitor I use for my son uses this same technology. Being able to see him sleeping so soundly gives me great peace, even in the dark of the night.

The thing is, we are really not afraid of the dark. We are afraid of not being able to see. So when we are able to see clearly, the fear of darkness loses its power. In the same way, when we allow the truth of God to light our way, we don't ever have to be afraid of how dark this world gets. Elijah sets this same example for us. He was not as concerned with what he could see as much as what he knew to be true of his Lord. In his encounter with Ahab, Elijah makes the point that his God "lives." That one small word is the very difference between the God of Elijah and the god of Ahab. Elijah's God can hear his prayers, see his troubles, and respond to his call. Although his God could not be physically seen like the idols of Ahab, that did not make Him any less real. In fact, God was about to show the Israelites just how real, capable, and powerful He was. Elijah did not need a physical or tangible false god when he intimately knew the True Living God.

Ironically, our physical sight can too often block our spiritual sight. So we need night vision. **We need the ability to see through the darkness of this world to see the things of God.** Our biggest problem with this is that we can become so distracted by what we can see in this world that we lose sight of the intangible truths of God that are just as real. When we do this we allow the darkness of this world to blind us of God's light. **So if we do not want to become discouraged by what we see, we must remain encouraged by what we know.** We must place our trust in the truth of God and not what we see. It is this faith that gives us night vision. It enables us to see that there is more to this world than meets the eye, and it empowers us to know the truth even when we cannot see it. It is important that we realize that our limited vision does not limit our God. No matter how dark it gets, He will always be the same able, powerful, and loving God.

When we do not possess the night vision that faith produces, we deceive ourselves into thinking that maybe God isn't as powerful as the Bible says He is. We'll say things like, "Jesus can't pay my bills," "Jesus can't hold me at night," or, "Jesus can't help me." But the fact of the matter is that Jesus is trying to give us more than we can see and feel. At the end of this life, this physical earth will not matter. What we see now will be gone, and our spirit will come face to face with the Spirit of God. For this reason the apostle Paul tells us:

> *So we fix our eyes not on what is seen, but on what is unseen, since what is seen is temporary, but what is unseen is eternal.* — 2 Corinthians 4:18

The darkness of this world will cause us to go blind if we allow it. On the other hand, when we place our faith in God and not only what we can see, we are empowered to see beyond our current circumstance. We then gain vision to see that God's light is always greater than the darkness, even when it doesn't seem that way.

WE ARE THE LIGHT

The Israelites' relationship with their God was as bad as it could possibly be. If we did not have night vision we might think there was no hope for them. We will see, however, that when things are at their worst, God shows up with His best. Isaiah 59:19 tells us:

> *When the enemy shall come in like a flood, the Spirit of the* LORD *shall lift up a standard against him. – Isaiah 59:19 (KJV)*

The Israelites were flooded with idol worship and poor leadership, but God was faithful to raise up a standard against it. Their dark situation was met with the greatest prophet of their time: Elijah. I believe God is currently raising a standard against the darkness you are experiencing in your home, community, and world. And beloved, you are that standard. **God's answer to the darkness around us is the light He has placed in us.** Darkness only exists in the absence of light, and as Jesus told us, we are the light. The brighter we shine, the further the darkness must flee. God is raising you up to be a Daughter of Fire who burns bright for Him, reflecting His glory and light to show the world that evil will not prevail.

God is raising a standard that the enemy has no power to ever defeat or overcome. If we are concerned about the darkness in this world, we must be reminded that we are the light! We hold the solutions to the problems we see around us. It's time to stand boldly, humble ourselves before God, and open our eyes to this truth: No matter how dark it gets, light always wins.

REFLECTION QUESTIONS

1) In this chapter we learned about the social, political, and spiritual environment Elijah faces on his mission to turn the hearts of the Israelites back to God. Think of your "now" situation–your current circumstances, the people you encounter every day, and how you live your life. Are you bold and unashamed for your God? Are people clear about the God that you serve?

2) Elijah was quick to give God glory when he first approached King Ahab. Do you humbly give God credit for what he is doing and will do in your life so that others may know Him?

3) The Israelites found themselves far from God because of their idol worship. Do you desire God, or do you run

from one earthly pleasure to the next? Do you sincerely believe that God is greater than what this world has to offer, and do you live like it?

PRAYER

Dear Heavenly Father, I pray for grace and strength to boldly serve You, to humbly praise You. And I pray for the spiritual vision to know and believe You are greater than what this world has to offer. In Jesus Christ's name I pray. Amen.

CHAPTER TWO

Extinguished: The Quickest Way to Put Out Fire

> *"It is too much for you to go up to Jerusalem. Here are your gods, Israel, who brought you up out of Egypt."*
> — 1 Kings 12:28

Have you ever witnessed a prominent pastor or Christian fall in the public eye, and said, "How did that happen? How can you be so seemingly close to God one day, and so far the next? So on fire today in the public eye, and completely extinguished tomorrow?" This is how I felt about the Israelites. I wondered how the very people of God, His chosen people, who His presence was with and who He spoke to, could find themselves the furthest from Him than they had ever been. We can find the answer to this question by looking a little deeper into their past to learn how we can avoid the same mistakes. Because if we are to be light in the darkness, the last thing we need is for our fire for God to go out.

I have to be honest with you. I was particularly convicted when studying the text for this chapter. God personally revealed some idols and lies in my own heart that I believe made me no different than the Israelites. So I want us to approach this chapter with humble hearts and a willingness to yield to the conviction from God about any idol we may have in our hearts. In doing so, my prayer is that we will be empowered, by God's grace alone, to tear down those idols, believe God's truth, and live lives solely for the glory of God. This is important because it does not matter how strong we feel or how long we have been saved. We are all susceptible to sin and being overtaken by deception and lies.

Speaking of lies, they are the enemy's greatest weapon against us. When Jesus was tempted for forty days in the wilderness, the enemy approached Him three times and attempted to prevent Jesus from completing the mission God placed on His life. Each temptation the enemy presented to Jesus was rooted in a lie. Jesus, however, was able to combat each temptation with the truth of God. He quotes Scripture to fight back the lies of the enemy, and it was the very Word of God that empowered Jesus to be victorious even in the wilderness. As we look at the Israelites we will see that they too have been presented three major lies, but instead of standing on the truth of God, they believe the lies—a choice that would be detrimental for generations to come.

HOW IT ALL STARTED

We know the Israelites are in a dark situation and far from God. Now let's look at how they found themselves in this position. We know that they have been led by a string of kings doing evil in the sight of the Lord and arousing His anger, each king worse than the previous. Through all this mismanagement of God's people, the idol worship and Baal worship starts with one man generations before Elijah steps on the scene. His name is Jeroboam, and he successfully leads the people of God astray for his own selfish gain with lies and manipulation. He plants three lies among the Israelites to produce the dark situation we learned the Israelites are in now.

Long before Elijah, the Kingdom of Israel was divided because the Israelites could not make a unanimous decision about who should be the next king. Ten tribes made Jeroboam their king in the Northern Kingdom, and two tribes made Rehoboam their king in Jerusalem. Previously, God had already anointed Jeroboam to be king of the ten tribes he is now ruling. But, Jeroboam still becomes fearful and insecure that he will lose these ten tribes. He believes that when the people of his kingdom travel to Jerusalem to sacrifice and worship there, they will decide to turn on him and align themselves with Rehoboam.

So instead of trusting God, he takes matters into his own hands and devises a scheme to prevent the Israelites from going to Jerusalem altogether. He tells them that Jerusalem is too far, and he gives them two golden calves to worship in the convenience of the Northern Kingdom. Jeroboam successfully secures his monarchy at the cost of leading the Israelites into sin and further from the One True Living God with these simple words:

> *"It is too much for you to go up to Jerusalem. Here are your gods, Israel, who brought you up out of Egypt."*
> *– 1 Kings 12:28*

With this lie Jeroboam is successful in leading the Israelites away from their God. It's even more unfortunate that many of the lies Jeroboam used to turn the hearts of the Israelites from God are present today, still successfully turning our hearts away from God and to the things of this world. Let's expose these lies so that we may arm ourselves accordingly with the truth of God.

LIE 1: IT IS TOO MUCH TO SERVE GOD

The first lie that Jeroboam plants is that Jerusalem is too far for the Israelites to go worship. He tells them, "It is too much for you to go up to Jerusalem." Jerusalem represented the place where God dwelt, the place where the Israelites could encounter His presence. It was the location of the Lord's temple. King Solomon was the one who built this temple, and once it was completed God spoke to Solomon:

> *"I have consecrated this temple, which you have built, by putting my Name there forever. My eyes and my heart will always be there." – 1 Kings 9:3*

The Israelites travelled to Jerusalem so that they could encounter their God and worship Him. Jeroboam makes this task seem overwhelming. Jeroboam simply places in

their minds that God is too far and the work is too much.
We need to beware of people who want to take away our
devotion from God, people who tell us we're doing too
much and try to make us feel bad for our devotion to
God. If they are anything like Jeroboam, they are trying to
deter us for selfish gain. It would be in their best interest
for us not to seek God. Either it makes them feel better
for their lack of sincere worship, or they know we will
stop doing something for them out of service to our God.

Still, Jeroboam deceived many with this lie, led
them to worship idols, and stopped them from traveling to
Jerusalem altogether just as he desired. But there were a
select few who did not fall for Jeroboam's scheme. The
Bible tells us:

> *Those from every tribe of Israel who set their hearts on
> seeking the LORD, the God of Israel, followed the Levites to
> Jerusalem to offer sacrifices to the LORD, the God of their
> ancestors. – 2 Chronicles 11:16*

Those "who set their hearts on seeking the Lord" were
not deceived. This was not simply about going to
Jerusalem. This was a heart issue. Those whose hearts
were for God went to Jerusalem. They had a heart for
Jerusalem before they even went there because they had a

heart for God. They believed God over Jeroboam, and the fruit of that belief was their going the distance to serve their God.

As God's daughters we must ask ourselves, *Do I serve man, or do I serve God?* Because when our hearts sincerely desire God, nothing is too much. If seeking Him means getting off of Facebook, getting out of an unhealthy relationship, changing the music we listen to or the people we hang around, then that is what we should do. My parents would always say, "A girl's gotta do what a girl's gotta do." If we have a heart for God, we do what we gotta do to seek Him because we value Him above all. We place God over convenience and what is easy.

Many will turn from God because they have been convinced that He is really not worth the work, the sacrifice, and the inconvenience it would take to truly and sincerely serve Him with their whole heart. These are the women who will find themselves furthest from God. Let's not be those women. Let's not look for excuses to not serve our God. Although there are many excuses, they are not enough. Let's not be deceived into thinking that anything could ever be too much for our God, because the truth is our God is always worth it.

LIE 2: GOD ALONE IS NOT ENOUGH

Next, Jeroboam makes two golden calves and plants his second lie by telling the Israelites, "here are your gods." During this time it was custom for other religions (false religions) to have idols. The idol represented their god. An idol was a symbol of the god one served, similar to how logos today represent a business, brand, or person. Many of the false religions surrounding the Israelites at this time worshipped idols in the shape of calves because calves were thought to represent the strength and fertility of their gods.[3]

Jeroboam takes a little pagan false religion and combines it with Israelite worship. They will have idols like other religions, but these idols are supposed to represent the One True Israelite God. At this point they have not worshipped another god, but they have made an idol for the God they have. They were in line with the first commandment to not have any other gods, but they blatantly violated the second commandment which directs the Israelites to not make any idols or images to worship. (Exodus 20:3-4) God made this command because an idol is a misrepresentation of Him because He has no visible form. I'm sure the golden calves represented the strength and power of God, but in no way could they encompass, contain, and represent all who God is. They were made by man with the elements God created.

Idols place God in a box by focusing on one or a few of His qualities, but the only one who can truly represent God is God Himself. Idols cause us to worship the blessings of God and not God alone. This causes us to not be content with who God is, and turn our worship from God to the idol itself. God does not want us having idols because He wants our hearts completely devoted to Him alone. Deuteronomy 6:5 tells us to "Love the LORD your God with all your heart and with all your soul and with all your strength." But, we cannot completely commit ourselves to God and idols at the same time. If we give our devotion to one, we will not have any to give to the other. To love God with our all means not having divided affections. God wants our complete devotion. He will be our only God and will not compete with idols.

Most idols are earthly things we believe we can get from God: money, certain relationships, and material gain. Some idols we feel entitled to, like health, status, time, happiness, and comfort (a big one). Prosperity teaching says that if you have much money you are blessed. Yes, God is the one who blesses us with money. But when we focus on the gift and not the Giver alone, money easily becomes an idol. It is an image we want to use to capture the essence of God, but it cannot and does not. God is more than money.

I also want to point out that sometimes the idols in our lives are not so apparent. As a new mom I struggled through sleep deprivation, low energy, and less time to myself as I am sure all parents do. But I started to allow that lack to take away from my joy. I thought that if I had more time, or enough money for a babysitter, or more energy, then I would have more joy or be more equipped to be the woman God was calling me to be. But those simple, seemingly innocent things were becoming idols. God graciously corrected me by lovingly showing me that more than sleep or money or energy, I needed Him. During that season, and even now, I did not get more of what I thought I needed, but God gave me more of Himself and showed me that with Him I had enough. He alone was enough.

Whenever we are in a situation where Jesus is not the solution, we may have some idols. If we are constantly thinking or saying, "I need more of _____ to have joy or to follow God's will for my life," and that blank is not filled with Jesus, then we may have some idols. The deceiving thing about idols is they can be the most noble of aspirations—education, success, ambition, anything really. They may even be from God, but we must always remember they are not God.

This can be a dangerous, slippery slope. Idolatry is not unbelief; it is belief in the wrong thing. We make something an idol when we place our faith in it instead of God. And this is what happened to the Israelites under Jeroboam. They started to bow down and worship the golden calf idols. They worshiped the idea of strength and fertility as a characteristic of God, but these are not God Himself. They were misled into thinking the blessings of God were greater than God alone.

We must not focus on what we can get from God. Our pursuit is not for the blessings of God, but God alone. Through the good and the bad, through convenience and inconvenience, wealth and poverty, sickness and health, God alone is enough and worthy of our sincere praise. The Bible reminds us:

> *Whom have I in heaven but you? And earth has nothing I desire besides you. My flesh and my heart may fail, but God is the strength of my heart and my portion forever.*
> — *Psalm 73:25-26*

The quickest way to put out the fire of God in our souls is to have idols in our hearts. We must take the idols off the pedestals of our hearts and place God as

> # THE QUICKEST WAY TO PUT OUT THE FIRE OF GOD IN OUR SOULS IS TO HAVE IDOLS IN OUR HEARTS

supreme in our lives, where He belongs. We do this by not being deceived into believing that anything in this world is greater than what we have in Heaven.

We hold tight to the truth that God is greater than our desires, our plans, and our life. **There is no room for idols in the heart of the woman who truly believes her God is enough.**

LIE 3: WORSHIP IS ONLY ABOUT LOOKS

After Jeroboam presented the calf idols to the Israelites, he wanted to make the worship look as real as possible. He wanted it to look as sincere as what the Israelites would find in Jerusalem, just to be sure they did not go back. So he built shrines, appointed priests, made sacrifices, and even celebrated festivals on dates of his choosing. (1 Kings 12:31-33) He accredited what God did for the Israelites, like delivering them from Egyptian slavery, to these idols. The religion looked sincere and real, but it was far from the truth and far from God. What makes this lie so dangerous, and maybe even the most dangerous of all three, is the fact that when we make worship only about looks, we may think we're doing everything right. But our hearts could not be further from God–worship on the outside, disobedience on the inside.

Nevertheless, Jeroboam sets up these idols and then makes sacrifices to the Lord. He sins against God by creating idols, and turns right around to offer burnt sacrifices to God. His sacrifices were not genuine because they were not from a heart of obedience. The Bible tells us:

> *"To obey is better than sacrifice, and to heed is better than the fat of rams." – 1 Samuel 15:22*

God wants us to follow His commands His way. We may be doing something for God, but if it is not His will then He will not be pleased by it. The Israelites decided to worship Jeroboam's way and not God's way. But it is important for us to remember that obedience to God is our sacrifice.

This worship and sacrifice by Jeroboam was more about looking a part than it was pleasing God because only obedience through faith can lead to true worship and sacrifice acceptable to God. We cannot please God while believing the lies of this world. God's Word teaches us:

without faith it is impossible to please God, because anyone
who comes to him must believe that he exists and that he
rewards those who earnestly seek him. – Hebrews 11:6

Jesus addresses this same topic in a conversation with a
woman He met at a well in John 4. This woman was
looking for satisfaction everywhere but God, and now
found herself facing the very Person she needed: Jesus.
However, she is skeptical about Jesus as He is Jewish and
she is a Samaritan, and it was taboo at the time for the two
to even socialize. She then brings up one of the major
differences between herself and Jesus. While the Israelites
believed it necessary to worship in Jerusalem, the
Samaritans, like this woman, believed it acceptable to
worship at Mount Gerizim (also known as the mountain
of blessing) where they believed Moses had once built an
altar to God.[4] Jesus clears all this up by explaining that it is
not about location and the exterior when it comes to
worshiping God. He replies:

> *"Yet a time is coming and has now come when the true*
> *worshipers will worship the Father in the Spirit and in*
> *truth, for they are the kind of worshipers the Father seeks.*
> *God is spirit, and his worshipers must worship in the Spirit*
> *and in truth." – John 4:23-24*

Before the coming of Jesus, worship looked like going to Jerusalem, and it was heavy in rituals and traditions. And those rituals served their purpose. But now that Jesus has brought salvation to all (Hebrews 10:10), God has sent His Spirit to dwell in us. The place of worship is no longer in a temple, but *we* are now the temple where the Spirit of God dwells. (1 Corinthians 6:19-20) Jesus tells the woman at the well that God is surveying the earth actively, looking for daughters who are worshiping Him in the Spirit and in truth.

You see, we can go to church, raise our hands, run down the aisle, and even speak in tongues, and still not be worshiping in the Spirit and in truth. I'm not saying to not do those things or that those things are not important, but the Bible tells us that without worshiping in the Spirit and in truth those things are not the evidence of true worship that God is looking for.

He is looking for worship not just in a spirit but the Spirit, meaning the Holy Spirit of God Himself. The only way we can do this is if we have received Jesus Christ as our Lord and Savior. At that point we receive the Holy Spirit and our bodies become a temple where true worship can take place despite our geographical location.[5] But our worship should not only be about feelings and emotions.

We must also worship in truth. A key mistake the Israelites made was that they listened to the direction of Jeroboam over that of their God. God is looking for daughters who will worship Him because they believe the truth. Why is it so important that we make every effort to grow in our relationship with Christ and in our knowledge of Him? Because we cannot sincerely worship who we do not know. This is not simply a matter of knowing about God, but knowing Him personally. We do this by seeking Him through prayer, reading His Word, and believing the truth that He reveals to us as we seek Him.

BELIEVING BETTER

Being a Daughter of Fire is not only about what we do, but also what we believe. God wants us to believe in Him because He is truth. And **believing the truth is the only way not to be overtaken by the lies of the enemy because lies cannot grow in a foundation of truth.** In contrast, we will not benefit from the truth of God and combat the lies of the enemy unless we actually believe the truth. All of our sin—all of it—is rooted in some form of disbelief. If the enemy wants to get us to turn from God,

> WE CAN'T START DOING BETTER UNTIL WE START BELIEVING BETTER

his strategy will be to tell a lie. Jesus tells us the enemy is the father of lies. (John 8:44) And we are constantly being lied to. Just turn on your TV or get on the Internet. The lie is big and loud and in our faces. It says we don't need God because this world has all we need. If we choose to believe that, then that is the direction we will go—toward the things of this world, just as the Israelites went toward the worldly idolatry of their time. However, if we choose to believe the truth that God is greater than this world and He is enough, we will find ourselves in His direction, just like the Israelites who went back to Jerusalem despite what Jeroboam said. I can tell you the truth, but believing it is up to you. The choice is yours to make, but know this: we can't start doing better until we start believing better.

REFLECTION QUESTIONS

1) In this chapter we learned that what we believe directly affects our actions and the lives we live for Jesus. What fruit do you see in your life as evidence of your belief in the Gospel of Jesus Christ?

2) The Israelites were deceived into thinking that worship to God was too much, that God alone was not enough, and that worship was only about looks. What are some lies you may have bought into? I challenge you to pray about these particular areas and study the Bible to shed God's truth over these areas.

3) God told the Israelites not to have idols because He knew they would hinder their worship to Him alone. Are there any idols in your life that may be stealing your affection from God?

PRAYER

Dear Heavenly Father, I thank You for Your truth. I thank You that through Your Son Jesus Christ I may know You and walk in light and truth. I pray You keep me and guard me from the lies of the world, that the light of Your truth will reap much fruit for Your kingdom through me. In Jesus Christ's name I pray. Amen.

CHAPTER THREE

Burn: Allowing Any Season To Refine You For God's Best

Then the word of the LORD came to Elijah: "Leave here, turn eastward and hide in the Kerith Ravine, east of the Jordan."
— 1 Kings 17:2-3

Has God ever taken you through a season of loneliness, isolation, or waiting? Maybe you are a stay-at-home mom drowning in diapers and a lack of adult interaction. Maybe you are sick and unable to get around as much as you used to. Maybe you are healing from a breakup or divorce. Maybe you are an empty nester or in a lonely marriage, an unstimulating job, a season of singleness, or you just moved to a new city or school. Maybe you are facing an isolating, slow, and restricting season in life.

For me it was 2014. Yes, girl. The entire year. My family and I had just moved to a new city, placing us farther away from friends. To top it off, I was pregnant and suffering from severe nausea. I could not get out as much as I would have liked and could not work on my ministry, Beloved Women, as much as I desired. I love to work, move, and get out of the house. This season restricted all of that. There were many days when I faced feelings of loneliness, boredom, and much frustration. However, it was during this time that I found much encouragement from Elijah because he too faced a very similar season.

When God first placed it on my heart to learn more about what it means to truly live passionately for Him, my mind immediately thought of Elijah. I was captivated by the story of his bold confrontation of the false god Baal, and God's coming down with fire to show He was the One True Living God. I mean, God laid the smack down on Baal! We will discuss that in more detail later.

But before all that, we find Elijah called to a ravine, away from the palace where he just left Ahab, alone and cut off from society. God has instructed ravens to bring him bread and meat in the morning and the evening, and he is to drink from a brook. Now, as miraculous as that sounds, when I read about Elijah's time by the ravine it all seemed so . . . well, boring. Nothing to do, all alone, and missing out on all the drama unfolding after the fatal prophecy he delivered to Ahab. You remember: no rain or dew for three and a half years.

Can you imagine how popular Elijah must have become during his time at the ravine? This is the man who boldly stood against Ahab and his false god Baal. Elijah's fame must have been growing more and more as time passed with no rain. Yet here he is by this ravine missing out on all of the excitement, so it seemed to me at least. But as we look closer at this time in Elijah's life, we will realize it was not a waste. In fact, it was probably one of the most important seasons of his life. It was at this ravine that we see God guiding, molding, and preparing Elijah for the mission he had been called to. We learn Elijah can't get to the fire until he has been through the ravine.

Which leads me to wonder, how many times do we think our ravine seasons are here to tear us down when they are actually here to build us up, make us stronger, and equip us for the call on our lives? Our seasons by the ravine are here to prepare us to be the women God has called us to be. God is not looking for perfect women. He's looking for daughters whose hearts He can mold, whose lives He can purify, and whose wills He can refine for His best. And since these ravine seasons are not biased, we all at some point must go through them, just like Elijah. So now we get to see the legendary prophet Elijah going through this refining process himself. It all starts after his encounter with Ahab with this word from the Lord:

> *"Leave here, turn eastward and hide in the Kerith Ravine, east of the Jordan." – 1 Kings 17:3*

In Elijah's season of preparation God directs him to do three things: leave, turn, and hide. I want to look into these three directives from God and learn how we can make the most of our ravine seasons.

LEAVE

The first directive God gives Elijah after his encounter with Ahab is "leave here." Elijah is to leave the palace and the presence of Ahab. God had not revealed to Elijah a complete laid-out blueprint of His ultimate plan for Elijah to turn the Israelites' hearts back to Him. Elijah is receiving one directive at a time, so he can only see so far ahead of himself. He has to faithfully complete each mission and trust God to then provide the next step. He must move forward not completely knowing where he is going. Yet, the Bible tells us, at the first directive from God to "leave here," that is exactly what Elijah does.

No questions. No hesitation. Just faithful obedience. In verses 3 and 4, Elijah is told to "leave," and in verse 5 we are told "he went." Now, if that were me it might have read more like "leave" in verses 2 and 3, some questions and complaining in verses 5 to 25, and then "finally Christina went" in verse 26. But not Elijah. At the word of God he leaves the comfort of the palace, not even waiting for Ahab's response. He does not lean on his understanding of how things should play out, but simply does what God called him to do. To leave a place or situation simply because God said so takes faith. Elijah could not see where God was ultimately leading him, nor how he would get there. He had no vision other than God's word, one directive at a time. However, God's word was enough for Elijah, and it is also enough for us. The Bible tells us God's Word is "a lamp for my feet, a light on my path." (Psalm 119:105)

Relying on and trusting God for each step in our lives is part of our refining process. It teaches us that His Word is greater than any plan. It helps us to learn that God knows what He is doing, and not to get ahead of ourselves. It helps us to ultimately stay on path, not becoming distracted with step ten when we have not even taken step three. With each step our faith grows and we experience the faithfulness of God on a very personal level, equipping us to take even more steps of obedient faith. And with each step God's plan for us becomes clearer.

Due to potential complications with my second pregnancy I received an early ultrasound. I was only a few weeks pregnant at the time and could barely make out the picture handed to me. It was a blur of black and white lines. As time passed, however, and with each ultrasound thereafter, the image became more and more clear. I could point out my son's nose, mouth, and even his little toes and fingers. But it took time to get to that point. In the same way, God's refining of His daughters takes time before His purpose is revealed.

How personally do I understand the struggle to want to know the clear, completely laid-out purpose of God on my life. I remember praying about my purpose in college and asking God to reveal it all to me so I could start working on it. I wanted to ensure I was heading in the right direction and completing the right major and internships. But God did not reveal it all to me because my desire to know His plan for me was more so I could work on it instead of relying on Him to bring it to pass. **I've since learned it is more important for God to purify our hearts for His calling than for us to simply know what it is.** If God had told me my freshman year at N.C. State that I was going to be a wife and a stay-at-home mom, I would not have known what to do with that. That was so far from my mind that I don't even know if I would have taken Him seriously. Yet here I am doing just that, and there is no place I would

> IT IS MORE IMPORTANT FOR GOD TO PURIFY OUR HEARTS FOR HIS CALLING THAN FOR US TO SIMPLY KNOW WHAT IT IS

rather be. It was not my plan, but as I have taken step after step of faith God is revealing His perfect plan for me more and more.

So I need to ask you: are you waiting for all the stars and moons to align before you decide to take that first step? Are you waiting for everything to be perfect before you answer God's call to do what you know He has placed on your heart to do? Well, daughter, that's not faith. I encourage you to step out on faith and go where God has called you. We may not understand, but honestly it's not our business to understand. It's our business to trust and have faith. I like how *The Message Bible* translation explains this truth:

> *Trust God from the bottom of your heart; don't try to figure out everything on your own. Listen for God's voice in everything you do, everywhere you go; he's the one who will keep you on track.* – Proverbs 3:5 *(Message)*

God is leading us to a place of preparation and refining, but more importantly He is drawing us closer to Himself. If God said, "Leave," His word is enough and He is faithful. We should definitely leave!

TURN

To be made pure, gold must be refined by fire. The gold is heated at very high temperatures so that it becomes a liquid. It is under this pressure that any impurities or foreign matter rise to the top to be skimmed off by a craftsman. The final product is pure and uncontaminated gold.[6] When Elijah was called to the ravine his faith went through a similar refining process. He was not only called to leave, but God's next directive was for him to turn. This meant there would be a change in direction. Elijah would literally need to position himself in such a way that when he left, the direction he was headed would not bring him back to where he came from. He would not only need to leave the palace, Ahab, and Baal worship, but also further position himself not to go toward it. When Elijah turns as God directed, it places him on the path to the Kerith Ravine. The name of this ravine means "to cut away" or "to cut up or off" in Hebrew.[7] God was leading Elijah in a direction to cut him off from the Baal worship and idols found at the palace. And that's what turning east did for him because that position led him straight to the ravine, the complete opposite of what he would find had he stayed at the palace.

Turning ensured his path would be straight—no zigs and zags like the Israelites in the wilderness. This would be a straight path right to where God wanted him to go. No distractions from the idol worship or defending himself against any naysayers. Following God is challenging enough, and we add more drama when we do not turn away from the idols God is calling us to leave. They entangle us and make our journey more burdensome than necessary. So when we answer God's call to leave we also need to turn from the things that are not of Him. **We cannot look back while taking that first step of faith toward our calling, and expect to end up in the right place.**

Even more than leave the palace, God wanted

Elijah to turn from its idols. God wants His daughters to do the same. He wants us to turn from the world and its idols. He wants to position us to be filled up by Him and not the false ideas of what we think we can gain from money, superficial relationships, prideful ambitions, attention from others, or any other thing we have made an idol in our hearts. **The beauty of our season by the ravine is that it strips us of these idols.** It's not easy. It burns, and we fight God and try to turn back because our flesh craves those idols. But under the refining fire by the ravine, our impurities are exposed as God skims them away to leave us with a faith more pure than gold.

The more we trust God by the ravine, the stronger our faith becomes, and we are able to see the truth about the idols in our lives: we don't need them. Even more, we learn and experience that God truly is all we need. He alone is enough. But oh how we run from this season! We run to social media, relationships, or work. We want to distract ourselves from the feeling of our flesh not being satisfied because it burns. **But if we would look to God and allow our souls to experience satisfaction in Him even by the ravine, that burning will bring light to a dark world and will testify to the greatness of God over every idol.**

God purifies and refines us by taking our idols away. Because how can we show the world that He alone is enough while we still glorify idols at the same time? That is impossible. So God calls us to turn toward the ravine—to turn away from the idols and show us that in light of His glory, idols are worthless and He is everything. How desperately do we need to behold this truth! **God is not stripping us of our idols because He is mad at us. He is doing it because He loves us enough to not allow us to continue down an empty path.** As challenging and painful as it may be, He knows the benefit far outweighs the pain. The Bible instructs us to:

GOD IS NOT STRIPPING US OF OUR IDOLS BECAUSE HE IS MAD AT US. HE IS DOING IT BECAUSE HE LOVES US ENOUGH TO NOT ALLOW US TO CONTINUE DOWN AN EMPTY PATH

> *Endure hardship as discipline; God is treating you as his children. For what children are not disciplined by their father? No discipline seems pleasant at the time, but painful. Later on, however, it produces a harvest of righteousness and peace for those who have been trained by it.*
> *— Hebrews 12: 7, 11*

How will we respond to discipline? How will we respond to the challenges of turning from the idols in our life? Will we get an attitude? Will we get mad and turn from God for asking us to do something so difficult in the first place? Or will we trust in His love, believing that He is not holding any good thing back from us? The decision to turn from our idols or not is the difference between the daughters who will simply *know* that God is enough and those who will *experience* His glory and sufficiency face to face.

HIDE

We've had to leave and turn, and that was difficult enough. Now comes the even more challenging part: we are to hide here. We are to stay here by the ravine. Being refined in our ravine season is never an easy process. It's not supposed to be. There is no quick fix. It takes time, and there are no shortcuts if we want to make the most of our time here. It's just like cooking chicken. If the fire is too high it will burn. If it's too low, it will be inedible. In the same way, the pressure we experience at the ravine will be just enough to effect lasting change. God is not going to put more on us than we can bear but he is also not going to allow us to stay the same. What is the point of leaving the palace, turning from the idols, and going through the ravine just to leave the same? The ravine is here to change us. The purpose of the ravine is to teach us, to train us to not rely on idols, and instead develop a complete reliance on God. This takes time, especially when we have relied so heavily on our idols in the past. So sometimes God calls us to set up camp and stay awhile.

I'm reminded of my first few days in Ghana, West Africa on a study abroad trip trying to adjust to the temperature change. I have never experienced heat like that before. One day while waiting in the van, I couldn't take the heat anymore. I was trying to adjust in my seat, hoping to find a position that was cooler. I was fanning myself and trying whatever I could to cool down. It was all in vain as the heat surrounded me and there was nothing I could do about it. I looked over to our translator who was sitting beside me, and she looked cool as a cucumber. She was completely unfazed by the heat, like we weren't even in the same Africa. When she saw my unrest, she laughed a little and simply said, "Be still." So I did. I sat there as still as I possibly could, and to my surprise she was right. I started to cool down once I surrendered to the heat, relaxed, and found rest even in my uncomfortable situation. Once I was still, I was able to find comfort in one of the hottest places I've ever been.

Both you and I understand how difficult it is to be still when life starts to heat up and the pressure is coming down. That is exactly what happens right after we turn from our worthless idols. It burns because we are waging war against our flesh and everything in us wants to run for relief. And in all that, God is saying, "Be still," sit right there, and let it burn. We're so confused when God tells us to be still. *You mean, do nothing?* we think. **Still, there are seasons when doing nothing is the hardest, most obedient thing we can do.** We must trust God in what He calls us to do and what He does not call us to do. God does not need us to do everything; He simply desires obedience. Sometimes He just needs us to be still and watch Him work. God tells us:

> THERE ARE SEASONS WHEN DOING NOTHING IS THE HARDEST, MOST OBEDIENT THING WE CAN DO

> *"Be still, and know that I am God; I will be exalted among the nations, I will be exalted in the earth." – Psalm 46:10*

God is not about busyness; He is about effectiveness. He does not need us working 24/7. Sometimes we will be more effective by doing nothing but simply trusting Him. How challenging this is in an Internet world where we have access to the entire world and anything our flesh may desire at our fingertips. So we need to ask ourselves, do we trust our actions and what we can do, or do we trust what God is doing? Do we trust God enough to just be still?

How many times do we find ourselves on social media, the Internet, or watching useless TV just to avoid our ravine season? How many times have we not trusted God to provide the strength to do whatever task we've been called to, no matter how mundane or boring it is? How many times do we not believe God will provide the good thoughts to think or prayers to pray in our stillness? So we fill our minds with useless mess to avoid the discomfort of feeling alone and being without our idols. Instead, we just find new ones to avoid the burn. But if we put away our idols and trust God in our stillness, we will see that He is faithful to His word. It was by the ravine that Elijah realized even in loneliness, boredom, and anxiety that God is enough.

Elijah had far more to gain by the ravine than with the idols of the palace. **We too have far more to gain in the presence of the Lord by our ravines than with the idols of this world.** We need more than what the idols offer. We need God. And we will find Him in our ravine seasons if we are faithful to stay awhile, get out of His way, and make room for Him to show up.

LET IT BURN

Many farmers burn their land to prepare the soil for the next harvest. The burning not only kills the weeds, but the seeds of the weeds as well. The next crop will be more lush and healthy than the one before. This is because this newer crop will not have to compete for resources with weeds. It will be freer to flourish like never before. In a similar way, our ravine season brings a purifying fire of its own—one that reveals where our true faith lies. The ravine lets us know who we are living for and who we truly worship. If we are living for ourselves the season by the ravine will destroy us. If we are living for God, however, the ravine will purify us. The Bible encourages us:

> *Blessed is the one who perseveres under trial because, having stood the test, that person will receive the crown of life that the Lord has promised to those who love him. – James 1:12*

May God's consuming fire replace the burning of our flesh. May we be strengthened to move from pain to passion. May we gain the burning passion that comes from knowing the One True Living God because we have followed His directive, turned from our idols, and have encountered Him face to face in every season. May we stand strong, hold on, and let it burn.

REFLECTION QUESTIONS:

1) God has called His Daughters of Fire to live for Him and not for themselves. Have you allowed God to control every aspect of your life, or are there still some areas you control without His guidance?

2) Elijah was called to leave the palace and central place of Baal worship. Have you ever felt God's leading to leave a certain situation or relationship? What was your response? Did/Does your response show complete trust in who God is in your life?

3) God calls each of His Daughters of Fire to turn from any idols in her life. This enables her to live for Him freely. Are there any things in your life that prevent you from completely following and worshiping God?

4) Think of a time you were in a ravine season. Have you ever felt alone, isolated, or bored? What was your response to being in such a season? Did you develop negative

feelings about being in such a season, or did you allow that season to draw you closer to God?

PRAYER

Dear Heavenly Father, thank You for the season I am in. I know that wherever I am, You are right there with me. I pray each season I enter will not be in vain. I pray I will be empowered by the Holy Spirit to allow every season to draw me closer to You and to mold me more into the image of Your Son. I love You. In Jesus Christ's name I pray. Amen.

CHAPTER FOUR

Fire: Making it Through Tests and Trials of All Kinds

"Now I know that you are a man of God and that the word of the LORD from your mouth is the truth."
- 1 Kings 17:24

I was in over my head. My family and I were so excited to move back home to North Carolina where we would be closer to friends and family. But our excitement was soon met with reality. My husband, Donald, took a job working nights so we could move back. It was best for me then to stay home with our one-year-old daughter. With Donald working nights our schedules did not allow for much family time. We were able to sell our home in

Maryland, but at a significant financial loss. We downsized our housing to cut costs, and things were tight. Months later, our apartment completely flooded and we lost thousands of dollars in property. Then, my dog died. Soon after that, my grandmother died suddenly and unexpectedly. Overwhelmed would have been an understatement to describe my feelings. I'm not sharing this with you to complain. I share these trials with you because sometimes we enter seasons of testing, one right after the other. It is completely overwhelming and frustrating, and right when you think you have your head above water something else rains down, making it hard to breathe. Have you ever been there?

Yet as difficult as tests and trials are, they do serve their purpose to ensure that our ravine seasons, discussed last chapter, actually change and mold us into the Daughters of Fire that God is calling us to be. So right after Elijah's season by the ravine we see a common theme: things seem to be getting worse as Elijah faces test after test. Elijah who was once provided water, bread, and meat by the ravine will now be provided only water and bread from a widow. Once in the safe and secluded ravine, he is now called to live in a Baal-worshiping area. Also, the effects of the drought had grown as time had passed, causing more and more people to suffer, including Elijah.

With a stream of trials facing Elijah we will see if he has what it takes to apply and live out what he learned by the ravine. To do so, let's look at how Elijah overcame each test he faced to inspire us in our own tests and trials.

WHEN YOUR BROOK DRIES UP

The first test Elijah faces? Running low on resources. Elijah stayed at the ravine for some time as directed by the Lord. After a while I'm sure he had grown accustomed to the miraculous provisions he received daily from the Lord. I bet he was quite used to the rhythms of his humble, daily routine. That is, until the brook ran dry and he had no more water. It was then that the Lord directed him to go to a town called Zarephath. There he would meet a widow who would supply him with food. I find it interesting, however, that the brook ran dry before the Lord gave Elijah further instruction. Can you imagine the days and weeks going by with no word from God as Elijah's water supply slowly dwindled? Yet Elijah did not run and try to find water elsewhere. He did not take matters into his own hands. He stayed right where God told him to be. And actually, the brook running dry was a good sign. It meant the drought God said would happen was actually happening. It meant God was a God of His word, and if He said there would be a drought, then there would be. It also meant that if God said He would provide for Elijah, then He would. Elijah prayed for this drought, and the dry brook was simply an answer to his prayer.

When we first moved to North Carolina, Donald and I discussed buying a house. But when we looked at our finances we concluded that a house was something we had no choice but to wait on. One night, however, I decided to pray about it. I asked the Lord to open up an opportunity for us to be able to purchase a house if it was His will. That very next morning our apartment completely flooded. The apartment above us had a pipe burst the same night I was praying, and the water flooded down to our apartment into every room except my bedroom where I was and where my daughter had snuck into my bed that night. That morning I woke up to Donald screaming my name when he arrived home from his night shift. I quickly got up and ran to the hallway only to find water everywhere. We had no choice but to look for a new place to stay. And to our amazement and God's glory, we found a home in our price range that was just right for us! The flood was devastating because we lost a lot of property, but I believe it was God answering my prayer. When we make requests of the Lord we do not know how He will answer those prayers or how they will affect us, but we can trust that He is faithful. The challenges we face are not all from the devil; some may be God closing one door so that He may open another. **Our challenges may actually be God working things out in our favor and answering our prayers.**

I love that Elijah did not take the brook running low as a sign that God had forsaken him. He trusted God and remained faithful by the ravine even when his situation got worse. Our trials have a way of bringing out our faith and testing it to see if it's real. In all our tests God is looking at our faith. He is not looking for us to be perfect, but to be faithful. Each test that comes our way is to see how much we will depend on Him and not ourselves. Will we follow Him even when things seem to be getting worse? When our finances, or patience, or hope is running dry? It was Elijah's faith that enabled him to place his trust in God and not the brook. It is by faith that we trust God and not our circumstance. Maybe your brook has dried up. Maybe you're not where you thought you would be in life, or have as much money as you hoped. Maybe your health is failing, your family going crazy, or the unexpected inconveniences of life are just simply overwhelming you. **These are not tests of our ability; these are tests to see if we will place our faith in God's.**

NEVER ENOUGH

Being in women's ministry has exposed me to some of the most prevalent problems facing women today. At the top of that list is the struggle of feeling like we are not enough. With so much pressure to do and be everything, many women feel inadequate to keep up with all the demands of life. There is just not enough money in the bank, time on the calendar, or energy in our bodies to keep up. These pressures are leaving us frustrated with ourselves, our family, and even God. Now, Elijah understands not having enough. We just read about his brook running dry. But I believe the widow Elijah meets in Zarephath can also completely relate to this type of pressure.

As directed by God, Elijah travels to Zarephath from the Kerith ravine. After his journey it must have been very pleasing to him to see the widow God told him would provide for him. Thirsty from his journey, he first asks the widow for some water. No problem. Without protest the widow makes her way to get some water for Elijah. But as she is leaving to get the water he asks for some bread too. She lets Elijah know she simply does not have enough. She says:

> *"As surely as the LORD your God lives," she replied, "I don't have any bread—only a handful of flour in a jar and a little olive oil in a jug. I am gathering a few sticks to take home and make a meal for myself and my son, that we may eat it—and die." – 1 Kings 17:12*

She could have just said, "No." But her words are dripping with frustration and resentment. When Elijah asked for bread this hit a nerve. After all, it was the God of Elijah who caused this drought, forcing this widow and her son to eat their last meal. Put yourself in her shoes. She's lost her husband and is now left with the weight of raising her only son alone. With this drought she has probably seen countless friends and family leave and pass away. Now she has accepted the fact that she and her son are going to do the same. Can you imagine why she would feel that she didn't have enough, and even that she herself was not enough? And here comes Elijah asking for more. Asking for her bread meant asking for her very last. How discouraged she must have been. But who better to encourage this widow than Elijah? He understands what it's like to run low on resources. He knows what it's like to only have enough for each day. He's seen God's faithfulness by the ravine and even when his brook ran dry. The faith he developed by the ravine was not just for himself. It was also for this widow. In the same way, there is someone who needs the faith we develop in our ravine seasons. There is someone who needs the lesson Elijah taught this widow: **fear is conquered with faith in God and His word.**

Elijah knew his provision did not come from the widow but from God. The widow was simply an instrument God would use to provide for Elijah. So Elijah tells the widow, "Do not be afraid." Instead of responding to her fear with more fear, Elijah responds in faith. I bet the widow must have been curious as to how Elijah could have faith in such a desperate situation since he was just as bad off as her, if not worse. Still, Elijah tells the widow to go on with her plan to make her last portion of bread. Then he tells her to give some to him first, and that the Lord will provide so her flour and oil will not run out until the drought stops. And guess what? God did just as Elijah said He would. Every day He provided for the widow, her son, and Elijah. Her oil and flour did not run out even after she gave what she thought was her last. Even when we feel we do not have enough or that we are not enough we can still give our all to God. He can do far more with our little than we can do with a lot. And that's what we see here with the widow. She gave Elijah a little bread, and God miraculously provided her and her son with food and water until the drought ended. She gave up her little to receive God's more.

Sometimes when going through tests and trials we feel we don't have anything left to give. But if we'll do our best, we can trust God will do the rest. Whether it's being nice when we don't feel good, tithing when money is tight, or following God when the desire to do so is lacking, we can

> GOD IS NOT ASKING FOR OUR PORTION AS MUCH AS HE IS ASKING FOR OUR FAITH

trust that if we give God our little, He can still do a lot. **God is not asking for our portion as much as He is asking for our faith.** This widow thought she needed water, flour, and oil. But what she really needed was God. And she learned that God is not limited by the things that limit us. What do you need today? What are you lacking and don't have enough of? **Remember this: we don't need to worry about doing, having, or being enough when our God is enough.**

TRAGEDY

Only seven months after being married to Donald, my mother-in-law, Valeria, passed away unexpectedly. This was a devastating loss. She was only forty-seven years old with big hopes for a future filled with many grandchildren. She loved children. Donald's response to losing her preached the Gospel to me more than any sermon I have ever heard. I watched his heartache and still his trust in the Lord even after such deep loss. He told me that even after her death he still knew that God was good, and that only He had the power to give and take away.

The loss of a loved one is one of the greatest trials we will face, one both Elijah and the widow knew about firsthand. Elijah lived with the widow and her son in the upper room of her home for some time after arriving in Zarephath. I imagine by now Elijah and the widow had grown accustomed to one another. I bet their bonds grew as time passed, and that they even had a daily routine. But the rhythms of their life were quickly interrupted when tragedy struck. The widow's son died.

The widow confronts Elijah and asks him why this had to happen. Blaming him and herself, she looks for answers, but there was no answer that could be given to correct the heartbreak of a woman holding her dead child at her bosom. So Elijah does not answer her questions. There was nothing he could say to make this better–there never is in situations like this. But Elijah does not decide to do nothing. He asks for the widow to give him her son, her only son. So with no answers to her questions, she gave up her son to Elijah.

It's a difficult matter to let go, especially of the things we hold dear in our hearts, and even more so to the people we hold dear. My friend Shade was raised by her grandmother Georgia most of her early childhood. She has fond memories of her relationship with her grandmother, and while growing up, the two were inseparable. When Shade was thirteen, however, her grandmother died of colon cancer. It was one of those defining moments in her life, one of those moments that affect you forever. For a child so young to experience such great loss is heartbreaking. I once asked Shade how she has grown from that situation, and the truth and wisdom in her response will forever stick with me. She said, "I learned that people are not ours. They are God's. We have no right to a person. We say, 'This is my husband,' or, 'This is my sister,' or, 'my child,' but in reality they are God's. He created them, and we are simply entrusted to the relationships we have with them."

Death is always a tragedy, and it's always painful. Deep down in our hearts we know this was never supposed to happen. And that feeling is right. We were made to be eternal beings. Death only entered the scene once Adam and Eve fell in the garden. Now we live in a world full of death, sickness, and pain. But we have hope.

God's ultimate plan is to create a new earth void of the things we hate: racism, slavery, illness, pain, and death. The list is endless. The Bible encourages us that one day God will:

> *'wipe every tear from their eyes. There will be no more death'* *or mourning or crying or pain, for the old order of things has passed away. — Revelation 21:4*

This is the hope we hold in the face of death: Jesus sacrificed His life for ours and overcame death so one day we will never see death again. How blessed we are to live on this side of the cross!

Elijah, however, never witnessed a resurrection. In fact, there is no record of anyone being resurrected from the dead before Elijah.[8] So as the widow gave her son to Elijah she had no hope to look back on and say, "God raised this person from the dead. He will do it for me too." Imagine her thoughts as she stayed downstairs, empty-handed as Elijah took the boy upstairs. **But we will soon learn there is no better time to be empty-handed than when we know the situation is in**

> THERE IS NO BETTER TIME TO BE EMPTY-HANDED THAN WHEN WE KNOW THE SITUATION IS IN GOD'S HANDS

God's hands. When we let go of our fears, even our worst fears, God takes them and does something we could never do. He uses them for His glory and our good.

Elijah takes the boy to his personal quarters upstairs. He lays the boy on his bed and prays for him. The Bible tells us he cried out to the Lord:

> *"LORD my God, have you brought tragedy even on this widow I am staying with, by causing her son to die?"*
> *— 1 Kings 17:20*

Elijah starts his prayer by pouring out his heart and cares before the Lord. He does not bottle up his feeling and concerns. He does not act like they do not exist. He does not pretend to be some super saint and continue on as if he has no concern. Elijah did not understand why God would allow this to happen. Why would He allow such a tragic thing to happen to this widow who had been so good to Elijah? His question was raw and real and true. There is nothing wrong with having questions. Actually, the Bible tells us to:

> *Cast all your anxiety on him because he cares for you.*
> *— 1 Peter 5:7*

God cares how we feel even when we do not feel well about Him. So let's be honest in our prayer life when we are hurt, confused, or even angry with God. Trust me, He can handle it. He would rather have an authentic relationship with us based on truth and honesty than shallow and superficial illusions. Being authentic and vulnerable with God allows us to grow closer to Him and to know Him more. And this is what we know about our God:

> *For we do not have a high priest who is unable to empathize with our weaknesses, but we have one who has been tempted in every way, just as we are—yet he did not sin. Let us then approach God's throne of grace with confidence, so that we may receive mercy and find grace to help us in our time of need. – Hebrews 4:15-16*

How comforting to know we can approach God with our tragedy because He knows what it is like to feel utter heartbreak. Like this widow, He knows what it is like to lose your only son. We do not serve a God who cannot relate to us. He stepped down from His holy throne to be one of us. He stepped out of eternity and into time to live among us and experience the good and bad of living life as a human. **For this reason, we can approach Him with** confidence that He understands our struggles because He is human, and that He can respond according to His will because He is divine.

NOW I KNOW

Once Elijah casts his cares on the Lord, he makes his request. He prays that God would return this boy's life back to him. Elijah prays for the boy three times. He seeks the Lord until He answers. Whether God answers with, "Yes," "Wait," or "No," is up to Him. But it is up to us to seek, to ask, and intercede like Elijah. The Bible then tells us God heard Elijah's prayer, and He returned life back to the boy.

What powerful things surrender and prayer are! The willingness of the widow to give up her son to Elijah's care and the faith of Elijah's prayer ignited the power of God in such a way that this boy's life was returned. It is when we surrender our lives and humble ourselves in prayer that God will use us to bring life and light to death and darkness.

Elijah carries the boy back down the stairs and gives him back to the widow. The widow holds her son in her arms, realizing for herself that her son is indeed alive. She then responds:

Now I know that you are a man of God and that the word of the LORD from your mouth is the truth. – 1 Kings 17:24

Some time had passed since the widow first met Elijah while preparing what she thought would be her last meal. Since then, God had faithfully provided, day in and day out. Neither her flour nor her oil had run out. Was that not enough for her to know that God's word was true? But what she may not have known before, she knew now. She now knew that the God of Israel could control more than her daily meal. He is more powerful than the weather. He is not equal to Baal; He is greater.

Before, she only saw Elijah's God for what He could provide. She appreciated having a daily supply of food, but that was the extent of her relationship with Elijah's God. She saw Him only for what He could give and do, but now she saw Him for who He was. The God of Israel is not simply a provider. He is the Provider. **To this widow He was once a meal ticket, but now He was everything.**

We sell ourselves short when we only see God as a life coach or a "Get Out of Hell Free" card. Yes, He can make our life here on earth better, and He does keep us from Hell, but we have missed the point if we think that is all there is to Him. We miss the point when we think we just want God, but fail to realize how desperately we need Him. We lose when we only want His benefits and don't see our deep need for Him alone.

We tend to want the temporary when God blesses with the eternal. We want happiness when He gives joy. We want riches when He gives inheritance. We want fame when He gives intimacy. We want knowledge when He gives wisdom. We are looking to God for the wrong things because we do not know Him. **Like this widow, we've confused His blessings with the extent of who He is, and we have watered down all that God could possibly be in our lives.**

So for His glory and this widow's salvation, God brings life back to her son that she may not only know about Him, but know Him personally. And God sent His only Son Jesus Christ to die on the cross, and raised Him on the third day. He did this not so we could live comfortably or think highly of Him, but so that we might know Him.

The widow saw God's power in her son being brought back to life. We see God's power in the resurrection of His Son Jesus Christ. This is how we know God, through His Son. This widow could now see what the Israelites could no longer see: God's true worthiness. She finally beheld His glorious might and power for herself, but soon enough so would they.

REFLECTION QUESTIONS:

1) Time passed as Elijah watched his water supply run dry, yet he still stayed by the brook as God told him. When things seem to be getting worse in your life, are you prone to do things your way, or faithfully obey and trust God no matter what?

2) Although the widow was faced with many negative feelings when she thought her life would soon end, she still woke up to collect sticks for her last meal. (1 Kings 17:10) This positioned her to experience a miraculous provision from God. Is there an area in your life where you are allowing negative feelings prevent you from moving forward?

3) Elijah's obedience to God was not only a benefit to him, but also to those around him. How has someone else's faith inspired and encouraged you in your walk with Christ?

4) The purpose of tests and trials in our lives are not to point out our inability, but to grow our faith in God's ability. In facing tests in your own life, how have you seen your faith grow in God?

PRAYER

Dear Heavenly Father, thank You for the hope, peace, and life You offer during the tests and trials we face each day. I pray You grace me with the courage and strength to endure to the end, and to finish strong that I might know You more. I love You. In Jesus Christ's name I pray. Amen.

CHAPTER FIVE

Light: Using Your Position to Advance God's Mission

Obadiah was a devout believer in the LORD.

— 1 Kings 18:3

So far in our journey with Elijah we've seen him boldly confront King Ahab, faithfully obey his Lord by the ravine, and be used by God to bring the widow's son in Zarephath back to life. We already have a pretty clear picture as to why Elijah is so legendary. His life has provided so many great examples that we can learn from. Some include being bold and unashamed for Jesus, trusting God apart from His blessings, and having faith in God's ability even in our weakness.

The more we get to know Elijah, however, the

more superhuman he may seem. The examples he set may start to feel unattainable. Up until now Elijah has spent much of his time away from idols and Baal worship. But what about those who were constantly surrounded by the abundant acceptance of evil? What about those who were right in the middle of the Baal worship but desired to serve God? Could they show the same level of faithfulness as Elijah? Over the past few years Elijah has been in hiding. But what about those who faced the struggles of living and working under the evil reign of King Ahab and Queen Jezebel? How were they to remain just as fervent for God as Elijah?

Perhaps you can relate? Maybe you are the only Christian at your job, school, or in your neighborhood. You are not alone like Elijah by the ravine, but you're alone in that you are surrounded by those who do not hold the same belief as you. They may even be hostile to what you believe. So the question arises: how do you remain faithful when you are the only one fighting to live for God? On his journey, Elijah meets someone who knows firsthand what it is like to live and work in an environment where he is the only one trying to serve God. His name is Obadiah.

OBADIAH

After his time with the widow, Elijah is called by God to present himself to Ahab once again. It's been three and a half years of drought, and it is particularly severe in Samaria. This is where we find the evil King Ahab. If you remember, Ahab had little to say when he and Elijah first met. But now, three and a half years later, Ahab has something to say. In fact, he has been on an extensive and active search for Elijah. He wants to talk now because the drought has hit close to home. When the drought started it most likely affected the less fortunate first, like the widow we learned about last chapter. So for the drought to have affected the king things would had to have gotten pretty bad. Three and a half years of bad.

It hit so close, in fact, that now Ahab, the king of Israel, was looking for grass to save his livestock. One might think he would order one of his servants to do such a simple task. But they have either died due to the lack of water, or they have left their king's side. Either way, Ahab is left to lead this task himself, and there is only one person both available and willing to assist—Obadiah. Ahab orders that they search the springs and valleys to look for grass, so they divide ways to search more ground.

Though he works for Ahab, we learn Obadiah is a

devout follower of the Lord God of Israel. If you think your boss is evil, you ain't got nothing on Obadiah. Obadiah works for a king who has aroused the anger and wrath of God like none before him. Still, the Bible tells us Obadiah was a "devout believer in the LORD" (1 Kings 18:3). Even more, it's not like he was working for Ahab and *then* found God. No, we are told he had been faithfully serving the Lord since his youth. He knew what he was getting into, and although he works for a government that supports the sinful and worthless Baal worship, he has somehow maintained his integrity as a servant of the Most High God.

Obadiah is a prime example that although we live in a dark world, we do not have to live our lives like the world does. So let's explore two main reasons why Obadiah was empowered to maintain his light for God in such a uniquely dark situation, that we may do the same.

USING YOUR POSITION FOR GOD'S MISSION

While in college I struggled with the thought that in order to glorify God and accomplish good works for the kingdom, it had to be done within the context of church ministry. So I taught Bible study, lead ministry meetings, and planned outreach events. I would get discouraged when school work pulled me away from ministry because I felt I was not doing enough for God. How far from the truth was I! In that season God showed me my school work was my ministry. If I did not do well in school and flunked out, I would not be able to minister to other students. If I did not go to class, take exams, or live in the dorms I could not relate to the people I ministered to. God was using school to position me to be used for His kingdom. Homework was just as important as Bible study. I realized God wants to use our current position to advance His mission. And this is exactly what we see Him doing through Obadiah.

Jezebel, furious about this drought, was now on a crusade to kill the prophets of the Lord. So to protect those who had not yet been found by Jezebel, Obadiah hides one hundred prophets of the Lord to save their lives. At this point Obadiah had advanced so high in rank that he now answered directly to the king. The resources this position provided meant he was capable of going three and a half years in a drought while still maintaining his own survival. That could have been enough for him. But he goes the extra mile and out of his way to save his fellow believers. Obadiah knows his position is not just for himself, but that God has placed him at the palace working for Ahab to accomplish a purpose higher than saving his own life. He uses his position to advance God's mission.

I'm reminded of Esther who was an orphaned Jewish girl who rose to be the queen of Persia. During her reign, the king of Persia honored a man named Haman and ordered that those by the king's gate were to bow down to him. Esther's uncle Mordecai, however, refused to bow to Haman. When Haman found out about his refusal and that Mordecai was Jewish, he set out with a plan to kill all of Queen Esther's people. Mordecai sent word to Esther about what was going to happen, and requested that she speak to the king to stop Haman's plan. Esther replied and let Mordecai know that if she approached the king without being summoned she would risk a punishment of death. Mordecai responded:

"Do not think that because you are in the king's house you alone of all the Jews will escape. For if you remain silent at this time, relief and deliverance for the Jews will arise from another place, but you and your father's family will perish. And who knows but that you have come to your royal position for such a time as this?" – Esther 4:13-14

God was the one who ordered Esther's steps to lead her to become the queen. Now she could try to use this position to save herself, or for God's purpose of saving His people. She chooses the latter. She fasts for three days and nights and decides to approach the king, and when she did the Bible tells us she found favor with the king. He not only spared her life, but also granted her request to save her people. An entire race of people was saved because she was not afraid to use her position for God's mission.

God has us at our jobs, schools, and neighborhoods to save people for His mission. We are not simply there for a paycheck or a title. There are people all around us whose souls need saving. They may not go to church, and they may not know God, but we do. God may very well have called us to this place to bring salvation.

Those one hundred prophets of God that Obadiah hid were dependent on Obadiah's ability to maintain his position working for Ahab. Their very survival relied on his dedication, expertise, and competency. He was not a priest, but his role was vital in God's mission to turn the hearts of God's people back to Him, just like Elijah.

This brings up an important point about secular work. Secular work is any position that does not work directly for the church. However, if you work in a secular setting this does not mean you do not work for God. Working in full-time ministry is not the only way that we can serve God. There is no need to separate secular from ministry when it comes to one's ability to be on mission for God. For this reason, Obadiah served God just as much as Elijah.

God does not call us out of the world. He has called us to it to be doctors, and teachers, and factory workers, not just pastors, missionaries, and Sunday school teachers. Nursing our babies, planning a conference, managing people, applying for an internship, washing the dishes, playing a sport— whatever and wherever God has positioned us—this is our ministry. We are called to do good works for Him right where we are.

> SIMPLY BEING WHERE GOD HAS CALLED US TO BE, DOING WHAT HE HAS CALLED US TO DO, NO MATTER HOW GRAND OR MUNDANE IT MAY APPEAR, IS OUR WORSHIP

Simply being where God has called us to be, doing what He has called us to do, no matter how grand or mundane it may appear, is our worship. We glorify God in the everyday tasks and rhythms of life by being obedient to Him. When we love God and love people, we worship God. And we can do that anywhere. God does not need everyone to be a Bible teacher or gospel singer.

He wants nurses, business owners, engineers, and stay-at-home moms. And to think of it, even Jesus was a carpenter.

God wants to send out saints into the world to be the light it desperately needs. So we can't live in Christian bubbles and make an impact for God in this world. We should not hide from the darkness of this world behind the walls of our churches and prayer closets. Rather, it is there in our churches and prayer closets that we should be empowered to go out and be the light. That might mean going to law school, moving to a certain neighborhood, or working in corporate America. God will use us wherever He has called us and wherever our obedience to Him carries us.

HONORING GOD'S AUTHORITY OVER MAN'S

While Obadiah was looking for grass as Ahab told him to, he met Elijah. When Obadiah realized it was Elijah, we are told he bowed down in reverence and addressed Elijah as lord. Now, politically Obadiah's rank and authority was higher than that of Elijah. But when the two meet, Obadiah is the one who honors Elijah. He is actually honoring God's mission through Elijah as greater than Ahab's mission for himself. He recognizes that although he works for the evil king Ahab, he ultimately works for God. The Bible tells us to do the same.

Whatever you do, work at it with all your heart, as working for the Lord, not for human masters, – Colossians 3:23

Obadiah was able to maintain his faithfulness to God while surrounded by much sin because he honored God's authority over that of man. When we work for man we can get discouraged and lose purpose and focus. But when we realize we are ultimately working for God, we can work with our whole hearts to please Him. When we feel unappreciated or unrecognized by others for the hard work we do, we must remember we are not working for them. We are working and serving for the pleasure of our Lord Jesus Christ who laid His life down for our salvation. If we have a position that others deem less valuable based on society's standards, we must again remember we do not work for them. We work for the Most High God. The also Bible tells us:

Better is one day in your courts than a thousand elsewhere; I would rather be a doorkeeper in the house of my God than dwell in the tents of the wicked. – Psalm 84:10

There is no better place to be than in service to our Lord. It is an honor to do the work of God. And God's work can be accomplished in any position and anywhere. The world puts a lot of weight on titles, authority, status, and salary. It's a big deal here in this world. People are quick to want others to know their rank and authority level. Many times this makes those in lesser levels of authority feel inferior.

As an intern I worked as a receptionist at the headquarters for a major bank in Charlotte, NC. This was my first corporate job, and I was so excited to be there. On my first day I was trying to figure out how to transfer a call, and I had no idea what I was doing. The lady on the phone then said something along the lines of, "I know you'll be happy when you get out of that job." She spoke as though my position was less than valuable. I could tell by her tone her intention was to make me feel inferior. I wish I could tell you that was the last time something like that happened throughout my working career, but I can't. I've worked as a receptionist, an assistant, and a secretary, and I've run across that kind of situation quite often. I'd be lying if I told you it never bothered me. After a particularly rough day at the office when my boss's boss disrespected me at a meeting, I came across this Scripture that says Jesus is *far above all rule and authority, power and dominion, and every name that is invoked, not only in the present age but also in the one to come. – Ephesians 1:21*

I was reminded that although I answer to an authority at my job, Jesus has been given **ALL** authority, and I ultimately answer to Him. And He does not lord His authority over me to make me feel inferior. He loves me, and He knows me. It was then that the people who walked around the office with their noses in the air didn't faze me at all. Actually, I started to pray for them because I realized they were placing their worth in a title or position. Because they did not know their value came from God, they needed to make others feel bad so they could feel good. But those who place their faith in Christ alone are free from this thinking, no matter their rank. Whatever position we have, we directly answer to the One with ALL authority—Jesus Christ. So it does not matter what others think of us or what level position we work. We can confidently work with our whole hearts to advance God's mission here on earth.

NO MORE HIDING

When Elijah and Obadiah meet, Elijah instructs Obadiah to tell Ahab he has returned. This completely frightens Obadiah because Ahab has been so desperate in his search for Elijah that he has made those who said they had not seen Elijah swear they were telling the truth. If it were found out they were lying, they would be put to death. Obadiah was afraid of this consequence. Remember, Obadiah was accustomed to hiding prophets. He spent the past three and a half years hiding the prophets of God, and he was probably prepared to hide Elijah as well. But now was not the time to hide. Darkness had prevailed long enough. Now was the time for light to shine forth. So Elijah comforts Obadiah and promises he will present himself to Ahab.

As we are positioned in a dark world to spread the light of Christ, we may be tempted to hide. But in light of God's ability, power, and love for us, we do not need to do that. So when God says, "Go, show Me to the world that they may know Me and follow Me," it is no longer time to hide. It's time to burn for Him boldly that others may find their way to God by our light. I know this is not a simple charge. I know it's hard. But as I've said many times before, darkness is where light shines the brightest.

And the darkness hates our light because our light exposes it for what it really is—a lie. **See, it is not our job to go around pointing out the darkness. All we need to do is be the light that enables those around us to see.** Our light shows that God is enough and worthy, and that automatically reveals that

> IT IS NOT OUR JOB TO POINT OUT THE DARKNESS. IT IS OUR JOB TO BE THE LIGHT THAT HELPS OTHERS SEE

anything apart from Him is not. So wherever we are, whatever we are doing, however dark it is, let's be encouraged to use our position to advance God's mission.

REFLECTION QUESTIONS

1) Obadiah used his position as Palace Administrator to help God's prophets whose lives were in danger. How can you use where God has positioned you—whether in work, school, or life—to advance His kingdom and purposes?

2) Obadiah honored God's authority over that of King Ahab's. No matter where you work or what authority you answer to, you ultimately answer to Jesus Christ who is over **all** authority. How has this truth affected your outlook on your current position?

PRAYER

Dear Heavenly Father, thank You for allowing me to be a part of Your will being done here on earth as it is in Heaven. May I obediently follow the example of Jesus wherever I go that others may know You and follow You. I love You. In Jesus Christ's name I pray. Amen.

CHAPTER SIX

Flicker: Turning Your Wavering Passion For God Into An All-Consuming Fire

Elijah went before the people and said, "How long will you waver between two opinions?" – 1 Kings 18:21

During my freshman year of college I decided I wanted to see what the college party scene was all about. One Friday there was a party in the Talley Student Center that night. I called my friend Sharde after classes to see if she would go with me. She said, "Yes," but reminded me that there was also a play being performed that night called "In and Out of Christ in the College Life." I remembered hearing good things about the play, and I wanted to go see it. We decided we would go to both the play and the party. When I called another friend to see if she wanted to join us, I'll never forget the question she asked me: "So you are going to attend the Christian play and then the devil Talley party?" I replied, "Well, it sounds bad when you put it that way." We laughed and she declined my offer. Sharde and I still planned to attend both. The decision was a reflection of my divided heart and wavering devotion to God. This is the same heart condition the Israelites had under Ahab's rule. They wanted their holy God *and* the evil false god Baal. But God had had enough. So He sends Elijah out of hiding to speak with Ahab again.

A lot has changed since their first encounter. Three and a half years into this drought and they have suffered the loss of crops, livestock, and people. Imagine the stench of death in the air. You'd think God had proven His point. You'd think Ahab would have realized by now that the Lord was the One and True God able to control the weather. You'd think Ahab would be ready to repent, admit the worthlessness of Baal, and worship the God of his ancestors. You'd think he would at least greet Elijah with some respect and courtesy. But he does not. When he finally sees Elijah after desperately looking for him all this time he calls him the "troubler of Israel." (1 Kings 18:17)

Ahab believes Elijah is the cause of all his trouble.

But Elijah, unafraid and bold as usual, reminds Ahab that this drought and all of the trouble Ahab and the Israelites are facing is their own doing. Although Ahab's encounter with Elijah is less than courteous, it is not as harsh as I expected. If Elijah was such a troublemaker, why not kill him right there on the spot? It seems Ahab was not willing to risk being wrong. He apparently was not as zealous for Baal as his wife, and not as devoted to the God of Israel as Elijah. Ahab clearly had a wavering faith. Whether he wanted to admit it or not, Elijah's God had caught his attention, so much so that at the command of Elijah he gathered all the Israelites and prophets of Baal together on Mount Carmel to hash everything out.

DECIDING MOMENT

Once assembled on Mount Carmel, Elijah asked the Israelites a very important question. The Bible tells us:

> *Elijah went before the people and said, "How long will you waver between two opinions?" – 1 Kings 18:21*

Now that Elijah has their attention, he gets right to business. The Bible tells us he went before "the people." Now, there is something very significant we need to see

here. Elijah does not go before the prophets of Baal. He
specifically addresses the Israelites only. This meeting on
Mount Carmel was about God getting back the sole
devotion of His people. It was not about God confronting
Baal. This was not an effort on God's part to flex His
muscle and prove Himself against Baal as the better God.
This was a personal matter between God and His people.
As far as we're concerned, Baal was a non-factor. He was
simply in the way of God accomplishing His mission of
turning the hearts of His people back to Himself. In fact,
Jezebel was not at this meeting. She didn't need to be
because she was not undecided about her devotion to
Baal. She was hot and zealous for her god. This meeting
was for God's people who were wavering between God
and Baal.

Elijah uses the word "waver" which in the original
Hebrew translation means to "limp" or to "pass over."[9]
Wavering in our faith causes much confusion and
indecisiveness, which leads to a weak faith walk with God.
Since what we believe about God is the backbone to our
walk with Him, our wavering only hinders our growth in
Christ. And when we do that we "pass over" or forfeit
all He has for us. The Bible tells us:

> *Those who cling to worthless idols turn away from God's love for them. – Jonah 2:8*

When we waver in our faith we cannot go far with God or the world. It's a waste of time. So Elijah confronts the Israelites about their wavering faith and clarifies what their two options are—God or Baal. Elijah words the choice this way:

> *"If the LORD is God, follow him; but if Baal is God, follow him." – 1 Kings 18:21*

Elijah does not say: "If God is convenient for you," or, "If God makes you comfortable," or, "If choosing God is easy for you, then follow Him." Elijah could have even said, "If God delivered you from Egyptian slavery," or, "If God parted the Red Sea and stopped the Jordan River," or, "If God brought you into the Promised Land, then follow Him." Elijah said none of that. God, in fact, did do all those things. But Elijah is making the point that even if God did not do any of that, He is to be served on the simple premise that He is God alone. **We do not serve God for what He can give us. We serve Him because He is God.** We serve Him because He is the all-powerful and loving Creator of all, and the forgiver of sins. If we believe He is all of that, then shouldn't we place our complete devotion in Him alone?

A decision has to be made because God is not willing to share devotion, worship, and reverence that is rightfully His. From the very beginning He gave us a choice. When He told Adam and Eve in the Garden of Eden not to eat of the fruit on the tree in the middle of the garden, they were given the choice to follow God's will or their own. When the Israelites were in the wilderness God gave them the choice to follow Him or not. God told them:

> *"I have set before you life and death, blessings and curses. Now choose life" – Deuteronomy 30:19*

When it comes to deciding if we will follow God or not, God has not provided a gray area for us. It's either life or death, God or not. The choice is ours. God made it simple for the Israelites and for us. He simply wants us to choose life by choosing Him. However, we cannot do that when our affections are divided. Joshua presented this same choice before the Israelites after they entered the Promised Land:

> *"If serving the LORD seems undesirable to you, then choose*

> *for yourselves this day whom you will serve, whether the gods your ancestors served beyond the Euphrates, or the gods of the Amorites, in whose land you are living. But as for me and my household, we will serve the LORD."*
> — *Joshua 24:15*

Joshua had decided.

When Mary chose to sit and listen to Jesus while her sister Martha was consumed with busyness, Jesus tells Martha:

> *"You are worried and upset about many things, but few things are needed—or indeed only one. Mary has chosen what is better, and it will not be taken away from her."*
> — *Luke 10:41-42*

Mary had decided.

Rahab had the choice to either protect the Israelite spies that she was hiding or turn them over at the command of her king. She risked her life to choose to side with the One True God. (Joshua Chapter 2)

Rahab had decided.

THE WASTE OF WAVERING

When Elijah presents this generation of Israelites with the same option, the Bible tells us that "the people said nothing." (1 Kings 18:21) The Israelites think it appropriate to remain silent. It is possible they were confused by Elijah's demand for them to make a choice in the first place. Baal was actually many gods who had different characteristics and qualities depending on the region in which he was worshipped.[10] So to worship both God and Baal for their convenience did not present a conflict of interest to the Israelites. But although Baal may have conformed to the wishes and desires of those worshiping him, the God of Israel would not. God tells His people to have no idols (Leviticus 26:1), serve no false gods (Exodus 34:14; Jeremiah 25:6), place nothing above Him (Exodus 20:3), and love Him with everything we have. (Deuteronomy 6:5; Luke 10:27) Such devotion cannot be attained with a divided heart. The Israelites thought staying silent would get them off the hook, but not choosing was a choice; it was the choice to stay lukewarm in their devotion to God. In the book of Revelation we read of a church that had decided to waver in their faith just like the Israelites. To them God said:

*I know your deeds, that you are neither cold nor hot. I wish
you were either one or the other! So, because you are
lukewarm—neither hot nor cold—I am about to spit you
out of my mouth. You say, 'I am rich; I have acquired
wealth and do not need a thing.' But you do not realize that
you are wretched, pitiful, poor, blind and naked."*
— *Revelation 3:15-17*

The worst thing about being lukewarm is we think we're
OK. We think we have satisfied God and that we have
somehow done just enough to appease His wrath for our
sin. But our salvation does not come from works but from
faith. It's not about if we've done enough; it's about if we
believe God or not. From
Genesis to Revelation the
question remains: will we
choose God? We do not
have the option to remain
silent like the Israelites
thought they could. It is
inevitable that we all must
choose. The Christian life is
not an easy one. Deciding to
follow Christ is one that requires self-sacrifice and total
surrender. At the same time, it is completely worth it. **But**

TO THINK WE CAN RECEIVE ALL THE BENEFITS OF SALVATION WITH A HALFHEARTED DEVOTION TO GOD IS TO BELIEVE A LIE, AND IT IS A COMPLETE WASTE OF TIME

to think we can receive *all* the benefits of salvation with a halfhearted devotion to God is to believe a lie, and it is a complete waste of time.

Like the Israelites, I was confronted with my wavering faith the night my friend and I decided to attend both the "Christian play and the devil Talley party." First we attended the play. It was entertaining and life changing all at the same time. It really had me questioning my devotion to God. At the end of the performance the writer of the play asked everyone to close their eyes as he presented the Gospel. He invited anyone to stand up if they would like to accept Christ as their Lord and Savior. I remember thinking, *I'm already saved. So glad I don't need to stand up.* But then he explained that some people in the audience were saved but had not allowed God to direct their lives completely. They had not given God complete control in the driver's seat of their lives. I thought about it and was convicted. I gave my life to Christ as a child and tried to be good out of obligation, not out of a sincere response to the Gospel. I lived a good, moral life because it was convenient for me. So when the writer of the play asked those who were not fully devoted to God to stand up to rededicate their lives to Him, I knew I needed to stand. I had accepted Christ as my Savior, but not my Lord, until that night. I stood and prayed a prayer of rededication to stop living for myself and to start living for God. When I opened my eyes I realized my friend Sharde was also standing. She gave her life to Christ that night. I didn't even know she was not saved. Needless to say, we did not make it to the party that night. We left with a passion to truly live for God with our whole lives, not just part of them.

We had decided.

FIRE FOR THE SACRIFICE

Since Elijah knew the Israelites were hesitant to make a decision, he responds to their silence with a proposal. He and the 450 prophets of Baal will prepare two bull sacrifices—one for Elijah and one for the prophets of Baal. Once their sacrifices were prepared they would not set fire to it. The prophets of Baal would call on Baal, and Elijah would call on the Lord God. Then the God that answered by fire would be honored as the true and only God.

The Israelites were unsure of whom they should choose to follow; however, they could not waver forever, especially if Elijah had anything to do with it. So this proposal from Elijah was appealing. It would provide just the sign they needed to make the choice that had to be made. What they probably did not realize was the brilliance behind this plan that God had instructed Elijah to propose. Elijah suggests a sacrifice accepted by fire. This sacrifice would be a key component in his mission to turn the hearts of the Israelites back to God. Although the Israelites were looking for a sign, Elijah really knew what they needed was a sacrifice.

Sacrificial offerings were not new to the Israelites. God instituted the ritual of regular sacrifices as a way to cleanse the Israelites of their sins so they might continue to have a relationship with Him. Sacrifices usually required the offering of their livestock or crops. It was a statement by the one offering that they were willing to give up their best to receive God's best. God accepted these sacrifices to atone for their sin, but they also served as a way for the Israelites to proclaim their dedication to God. The sacrifice Elijah is proposing would represent the first steps that needed to be taken to mend their broken commitment to God. We also have that same opportunity. But instead of providing sacrifices like the Israelites, Jesus Christ stepped in to be our sacrifice. In Romans we read that Jesus is our "sin offering" (Romans 8:3) so that we may be reconnected to God.

This gives me chills because after studying how

Israelite offerings were prepared for sacrifice, I now know how gruesome they were. The priests were to slaughter the animal offering a certain way. They were to cut it into pieces and place some or all of it on the altar.[11] I have the luxury of buying meat nicely packaged at our local grocery store, so I do not see the gruesome realities of butchering an animal. It's easy for me to take for granted the loss of animal life because I only see the end product. But the sacrifice Elijah would prepare would be a bloody and ghastly representation of how bad our sin is. It would serve as a reminder of how much of a mess we have caused by our unwillingness to follow God. And here in Romans we are told God sacrificed His very own Son as a sin offering for us. **If God did all that to provide a permanent solution for the sin that gets in the way of us having a relationship with Him, then it shows how desperate He is to have a relationship with us.** It is by His passion for us alone that we are saved from our sins. If He did not want us, there is no way we could ever establish a relationship with Him. **The foundation of our ability to be saved by faith in Jesus Christ is the fact that God wanted to save us in the first place, not that we simply wanted to be saved. We are saved by God's desire, not our own.** The apostle John encourages believers in the security of their salvation with these words:

> *This is love: not that we loved God, but that he loved us and*
> *sent his Son as an atoning sacrifice for our sins. And so we*
> *know and rely on the love God has for us.*
> *— 1 John 4:10,16*

God loves us and He reveals that love to us through His
Son Jesus Christ. We know God by knowing Jesus, and we
rely on His love for our salvation. We do not rely on our
love or what we can do for God, but only on what He has
already done for us. What does that mean for us today?
That means we have assurance of our salvation
because our salvation is based on God's unchanging
love and not our weak ability to love Him. We do not
need to fear because not only does God love us, but He
acted on His love to provide a way for us to know Him.

The passion we need to be consumed by is not
our own; it's God's. We could never love Him if He
did not first love us. The Israelites could have never
turned back to God if God had not first sent Elijah to
open a way for that to happen. John summarizes this truth
with these words:

> *We love because he first loved us. — 1 John 4:19*

If God is not passionate about us, our passion for Him does not matter. If God does not love us, our love for Him does nothing. If God is not on fire for us, any spark we have for Him will quickly dissipate. So there is no need to be discouraged because God is passionate about us. He does love us, and He is on fire for us! That is good news.

If Elijah's sacrifice was consumed by Heaven's fire, it would not only prove to be a miraculous sign that God is real; it would serve as a message that He desired His people, that He wanted them, and that their unfaithfulness had not extinguished His faithfulness. The same is true for us today. Although we have turned from God and gone our own way—intentionally and unintentionally sinning against Him over and over again—He still desires us, He still wants us, and He still burns for us.

The sacrifice has already been made on our behalf. There is no need to "get right" before we choose God. There is no need to wait until we start going to church, or reading our Bible, or stop smoking, or fornicating, or cheating, or cursing, or drinking, or any other excuse we come up with before we choose the Lord God. Christ came for sinners. God is not waiting for us to do

> GOD IS NOT WAITING ON US TO GET BETTER; HE IS WAITING ON US TO CHOOSE HIM

better. He has already decided that He wants us. The Israelites wanted a sign. For us, the cross is our sign that the God of the universe has already prepared a way to be in relationship with us by sacrificing His very own Son. This is the sign that God is on fire for us. We are desired, we are loved, and God is hot on our trail. He simply wants our hearts. **God has done His part. He has proven His love. He is not waiting on us to get better; He is waiting on us to choose Him.** So then, how long will we waver between two options?

REFLECTION QUESTIONS

1) The Israelites did not see anything wrong with worshiping both God and Baal. When confronted to decide which God they would serve, they remained silent. They did not realize that not choosing was a choice—the choice to stay lukewarm and double minded. Is there anything or anyone in your life that you worship other than God that is causing you to be lukewarm and waver in your faith?

2) Elijah insists that the Israelites cannot stay silent on the matter, and they must choose between God and Baal.

Have you decided to follow God completely and give Him total control over your life?

3) This chapter we learned that being a Daughter of Fire is less about our passion for God and more about His passion for us. Do you find yourself trying to work for God's approval, or are you resting in the finished work of Jesus Christ on the cross?

PRAYER

Dear Heavenly Father, if I have been wavering in my decision to completely follow and worship You alone, please forgive me. Your love for me is perfect, and You are worthy of my devotion. I choose You. I love You. In Jesus Christ's name I pray. Amen.

CHAPTER SEVEN

Consumed: Igniting God's Fire to Burn Bright Through You

Then the fire of the LORD fell and burned up the sacrifice, the wood, the stones and the soil, and also licked up the water in the trench. — 1 Kings 18:38

My great grandmother Geneva was a God-fearing woman. We affectionately called her Little Grandma due to her petite stature. When I was a child, my mother, grandmother, and I would visit her at her rest home every other weekend. We were four generations of women shopping, eating, laughing, and creating lasting memories. Before we would leave Little Grandma's rest home she would always give me a few coins and even a dollar if I was lucky. She faithfully read her Bible and walked to church every Sunday. We knew she enjoyed service when she bragged about "jumping the benches." That meant she experienced the Lord's presence to the point of shouting. My Grandma Ruby was also a woman of faith. She was a proud member of Calvary Baptist Church in Gastonia, NC much of her life. She was a mother of the church, sang on the choir, and served forty years on the usher board.

My mom never wanted to push church on me. We did not attend every church meeting or activity, but we were there faithfully every Sunday where I watched her worship, praise God, and cry out to the Lord despite her situation. I come from a strong lineage of women who both faithfully served and personally knew the Lord. But that fact alone would not be enough for me to know the Lord myself. After rededicating my life to Christ I started to sincerely seek Him. I started praying and reading my Bible out of a desire to know and experience God on my own.

I remember reading the book of Acts and learning how all the believers gave their very lives for the sake of Christ. They had a passion and fire for God that would give up everything for Him. It was a testament to me that Jesus Christ really was that worthy, and I desperately wanted to know God on that level. I didn't want to hear what others knew; I wanted to know firsthand for myself. As I asked, prayed, and sought after the Lord, He was faithful to reveal Himself to me so I could know Him personally. And knowing God for myself was the fire I needed to burn for Him.

If we want to live passionate lives for God, there comes a point in our lives when our faith in Christ has to be our own. If we want to live on fire for God we can't simply experience Him through someone else. **We can't burn bright for God with someone else's fire.**

This is an important lesson the Israelites were about to learn. Their ancestors had experienced God delivering them from Egyptian slavery, parting the Red Sea, stopping the Jordan River, and bringing down the walls of Jericho. But that was not enough. This generation of Israelites were privileged to come from a long line of people who witnessed the greatness of God. But now it was time for their knowledge of God to go further than simply what they heard happened to their ancestors. They would now experience Him personally for themselves. They would not have to look to the past for what God did for someone else. They would now have their own testimony.

FALSE PROPHETS

In order to make our faith our own we must determine the real from the fake. Elijah's proposal to determine who was the true God would do just that for the Israelites. Elijah and the prophets of Baal would both prepare a sacrifice and call on their God to provide fire for the sacrifice. The God who answered by fire would be considered the One True God. The prophets of Baal went first and did just as Elijah proposed. They called on Baal for fire from morning until noon, but nothing happened. They then started to shout and dance, but there was no response. At this point, Elijah starts to taunt them. He sarcastically tells them Baal must be sleeping or busy, and they need to shout louder. So that's exactly what they do. They frantically shout and dance, and even cut themselves.

They thought maybe the blood of the bull was not enough. They thought if they poured their very own blood on the altar it might grab Baal's attention. Elijah knew all this was a waste of time. Yet he waited patiently all day long. As the day went on, the prophets of Baal became more desperate. They thought their actions and works would move Baal. So the Bible tells us they became frantic. I mean, can you imagine how loud it was? If one person was screaming, dancing, and cutting themselves it would make for a scene. But there were hundreds of them doing all that. Imagine the noise, the sight, the gruesome mess. Then it all stops. Now imagine the contrast. All of their frantic worship met with complete silence, a silence that spoke volumes. The Bible makes a significant point to stress Baal's response to the frantic worship of his prophets—there was none. We are told:

> *But there was no response, no one answered, no one paid attention. — 1 Kings 18:29*

The only noise left was the sound of Baal's prophets panting, trying to catch their breath, and wondering where their god was. They were now as quiet as their god. The Israelites learned a very important lesson that day. No matter how loud we get, a false god cannot hear, see, or respond to us. We all learn an important lesson from this pitiful scene: **we will never find satisfaction in a god that does not exist.**

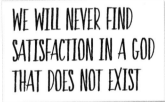

WE WILL NEVER FIND SATISFACTION IN A GOD THAT DOES NOT EXIST

Worship, no matter how grand, does nothing for a god that is not real. What is the point of living a passionate and on-fire life for something that's not real? Yet, this will be one of our biggest temptations. We are surrounded by those who want to usher us into worshiping powerless idols. And if we don't know the truth about our God for ourselves, we may fall victim to worshiping the lies of this world.

The prophets of Baal represented Baal and spoke on his behalf, yet Baal did not speak to them. They lived lives to give attention to Baal, yet Baal did not pay them any attention. They believed in Baal, yet their faith was met with no response. When I think about the prophets of Baal, they remind me so much of the entertainers that we flock to today—the music we listen to, the people we follow on social media, and the entertainment we allow on our televisions, computers, and smartphones. They all do a great job at making us believe the idols of this world can do for us what only God can do. Sometimes they are explicit and blatantly not of God. Other times the messages are more subtle. There might not always be cursing and misogynistic lyrics by artists and entertainers today, but some important questions still remain. Do they glorify money and material gain? Do they glorify pleasing the desires of our flesh? Do they promote self over God? Ultimately, we must ask ourselves, *Am I allowing this person to usher me into worshiping the things of this world? Do they increase my appetite for money, fame, and/or worldly pleasure over God?*

The job of the prophets of Baal was to inspire and encourage the worship of their god, and the same still happens today. We may not call them prophets, but we need to be aware of who we allow to influence and excite us. Even more so, we need to be cautious of where they are directing our attention. The prophets of Baal did much to attract attention to their god with all their chaotic screaming, dancing, and cutting. All of that drama to point to a god that did not hear, care, or respond. Like the prophets of Baal, the prophets of this world excite us to the point of exhaustion only to direct us to nothing at all. But when we know God personally, we can clearly see the real from the fake.

COME NEAR AND REMEMBER

Now that the Israelites had witnessed the truth about Baal, it was time for them to see for themselves why their ancestors worshipped the Lord God. After the prophets of Baal wasted all day with their worthless worship to Baal, Elijah had a small window of daylight to request fire from His God. Elijah tells the Israelites to "come near to me." (1 Kings 18:30 ESV) If they wanted to experience God for themselves, they would need to draw close. If we want to see God alive and active in our lives,

James tells us we need to:

> *Draw near to God, and he will draw near to you.*
> — *James 4:8 ESV*

Drawing near to God is not trying to work for our salvation. It's not the frantic worship that we see from the prophets of Baal. Drawing near to God is opening our eyes to see who He already is in our lives. It's opening our hearts to experiencing God for ourselves. Sometimes we block God out of our hearts because we're afraid to let God in our lives. We're afraid to trust Him, or we're scared that if we draw near we will be rejected or hurt. But when we harden our hearts in an effort to prevent ourselves from hurt, we block ourselves from ever truly knowing God. That's a high price to pay because we can't experience God if we don't know Him.

The more I've drawn near to God, the more I've experienced Him in my life. The more I pray, the more I realize He hears me. The more I read my Bible, the more I realize how true and unchanging He is. The more I choose to trust Him, the more I've miraculously witnessed His faithfulness. If we want to know God we must draw near to Him or we will never find what we are not looking for.

So in drawing near, Elijah is preparing the Israelites

to experience their God. But before preparing his sacrifice, Elijah rebuilds an altar on Mount Carmel that had been destroyed. In all the Israelites' wavering and double-mindedness, this altar was completely torn down as if there was no use for it anymore—until today. The loss of this altar represented the loss of intimacy with the Lord God that the Israelites had incurred as a result of their worship to Baal. The sacrifices at this altar would have served as a time to reverence God, and to remember who He was to them and all He had done for them. It was a time to remember His grace, mercy, and everlasting love. But because the sacrifice on this altar was abandoned, so was their remembrance of the true God they once served. So in his efforts to help them remember, Elijah repairs the altar. I want you to know that if you have found yourself far from God like the Israelites, now is a good time to remember who He is and Who you are turning from. **It is in our forgetfulness that our fire for God dims.** The Bible tells us to:

> *Praise the LORD, my soul,* **and forget not** *all his benefits. – Psalm 103:2 (emphasis mine)*

We will never honor and reverence God for His benefits if we forget about Him. Maybe you have broken your fellowship with God. Maybe you've been distracted by the things of this world and have forgotten about God. Well, now is the time to repair, remember, and ready ourselves to see God in our lives like never before. **Just like the broken altar Elijah rebuilt, God can still use the broken pieces of our lives to make something beautiful for His glory.**

After rebuilding the altar and preparing the sacrifice, Elijah further disadvantages himself by having

> **GOD CAN STILL USE THE BROKEN PIECES OF OUR LIVES TO MAKE SOMETHING BEAUTIFUL FOR HIS GLORY**

water poured all over the sacrifice, the altar, and into a trench he dug around the altar. Elijah sets out to prove just how great, able, and worthy his God is. **He knew a disadvantage to himself was not a disadvantage to his God. In fact, it would make room for God to show up in an even bigger way.** This would also leave little room for speculation or doubt when Elijah's God would answer by fire. This would be no coincidence. This fire would be an intentional act of God alone. By answering one simple prayer, what was once abandoned to forgetfulness would now be reestablished.

CONSUMED

"You got to get the fire!" the speaker yelled at us. I had the opportunity to attend the She Speaks conference in Concord, NC. This conference helps Christian women develop their writing and speaking skills. I wanted to attend this conference since the first time I heard about it, and finally my dream came true the summer of 2015.

My first session was titled "How To Get Better Bookings," and out of the fifteen-plus sessions I attended, this was the one that will forever stand out in my mind. The instructor told us that if we want to be speakers who get booked we had to get the fire. She explained that people are not coming to simply see and hear us speak. They want an encounter with God. They want to feel God use our words to stir up an awareness of His presence. And the only way we could do that is if we've experienced Him ourselves. We can use all the right lingo and speak with the finest eloquence, but if our words are not laced with the passion and boldness that comes from being in the very presence of God, they will be meaningless.

Actually, the same is true for all that we do. If we are not filled with the fire and passion of the Holy Spirit, we are not living in all the power and boldness God has for us. Like Elijah's sacrifice we can have all the right ingredients, but if we don't have the fire it means nothing. So there is no question about it. We got to get the fire! But how do we actually get this fire? Where do we get this burning passion for God that fuels us to do and be all He's calling us to do and be? It's simple. We ask for it.

When Elijah makes his request to God for fire we do not see any frantic worship from him to move his God like we did from the prophets of Baal. He does not shout, or dance, or even offer one drop of blood. He knows that fire from Heaven is not up to him. He understands it's not about his works, but God's. So Elijah does what he's always done. He prays. It is not even a long-drawn-out prayer. He does not use a lot of words and big vocabulary. It is a simple, two-sentence prayer that yields powerful results. He prays:

> *"LORD, the God of Abraham, Isaac and Israel, let it be known today that you are God in Israel and that I am your servant and have done all these things at your command. Answer me, LORD, answer me, so these people will know that you, LORD, are God, and that you are turning their hearts back again. – 1 Kings 18:36-37*

You know what really sticks out to me about this prayer? Elijah wanted fire for the sacrifice, but not once in either sentence does he specifically say, "Lord, bring fire down." Instead, twice he prays that the Israelites would *know* that the Lord was God. Ultimately, all of this was about the Israelites knowing their God. If we want the fire we simply need to be praying for God to reveal Himself to us so that we might know Him personally. If we want to know how God responds to this type of request, we can simply look at how God responds to Elijah's. The Bible tells us:

> *Then the fire of the LORD fell and burned up the sacrifice, the wood, the stones and the soil, and also licked up the water in the trench. – 1 Kings 18:38*

Not only does God come down with fire, but He answers with a fire that consumes the entire altar. Even the stones are consumed. Can you imagine that? God comes through far beyond expectation. He could have just burned the bull offering. He could have simply burned the bull and the wood. Remember, they were already soaking wet from the vast amount of water Elijah had ordered to be poured on and around the altar. But God burns everything, even the soil and stones. There is no doubt that this fire was God's fire. I wonder, did Elijah and the Israelites feel the heat from the fire as it came down? I wonder, did the force from the fire push them back a little? I wonder how wide their eyes must have been once they saw that the entire altar was gone. No one, and I mean no one, but God could have done this. The Bible tells us:

*When all the people saw this, they fell prostrate and cried,
"The LORD—he is God! The LORD—he is God!"*
— 1 Kings 18:39

All along, the Israelites wanted water due to the drought, but what they received was even better. They got the fire. They received a fresh revelation of the presence and power of their God so great it's like God had been anxious to release it. It was like He was excited that the time had finally come for the Israelites to see His power. And we can trust that God is anxious to consume us with passion and fire for Him by revealing Himself to us.

THE FAITH TO ASK

While Jesus was on His way to heal a young girl, a woman with an issue of blood heard that Jesus was near. After twelve years of suffering from her illness, spending all she had on doctors and only getting worse, she believed Jesus could help her. She said to herself, "If I just touch his clothes, I will be healed." (Mark 5:28) She pushed her way through a crowd to get to Jesus with the little strength she had, and touched Him. When she did, she was then immediately healed.

What I love the most about this woman is her incredible faith. She never saw any of Jesus' miracles. She only *heard* about what He did. She could have thought, *Oh Jesus healed Sally. Good for her.* Or, *Jesus restored Jessica's sight. Must be nice.* Or, *Kelly was brought back to life. I'm so happy for her.* But she did not just believe what Jesus did for others. She took it a step further and believed Jesus could do it for her as well.

The Israelites needed this faith. They had heard of God's involvement with their ancestors, but they never truly believed they would experience Him in the same way. Sometimes when we see someone else on fire for God we think they are special and must have something that we do not. But God's not holding back His presence for a select few. He's ready to give the fire to His daughters who have the faith to be bold enough to ask for it. Jesus tells us:

> *"Ask and it will be given to you; seek and you will find; knock and the door will be opened to you. For everyone who asks receives; the one who seeks finds; and to the one who knocks, the door will be opened. Which of you, if your son asks for bread, will give him a stone? Or if he asks for a*

> *fish, will give him a snake? If you, then, though you are evil,*
> *know how to give good gifts to your children, how much more*
> *will your Father in heaven give good gifts to those who ask*
> *him!" – Matthew 7:7-11*

Just like the woman with the issue of blood, we can't allow fear to prevent us from seeking God. It's the only way we will get the fire. God desires to give us good things, and the best thing He has given us is Himself. **God wants to consume us with His fire more than we want it, but He will not force or impose His will on us. We must desperately want it, faithfully seek it, and boldly ask for it.**

REFLECTION QUESTIONS

1) The prophets of Baal worked hard to gain their god's attention, but we've learned this is not necessary with the Lord God who already came to us through His Son Jesus Christ. Do you work to gain God's approval, or are your works for God done out of a sincere response to what He has already done for you through His Son Jesus Christ?

2) We also learned that God goes the distance for His people. No matter how far away they find themselves, they are never out of God's reach. Have you found yourself distant from God?

3) From a sincere, two-sentence prayer we see God answers Elijah's request with consuming fire. Throughout the testimony of Elijah, we clearly see the power of prayer. Is prayer an important part of your life? Do you pray with an expectant heart that God hears and will answer you? Is prayer your first response to desperate situations?

<u>PRAYER</u>

Dear Heavenly Father, thank You for Your passion for me. Thank You for sending Your Son to die that I might know You. I pray I live a life that responds to the ultimate sacrifice of Your Son for my salvation with reverence, awe, and thanksgiving. I love You. In Jesus Christ's name I pray. Amen

CHAPTER EIGHT

Ablaze: Keeping Your Fire Burning For the Long Run

The power of the LORD came on Elijah and, tucking his cloak into his belt, he ran ahead of Ahab all the way to Jezreel.
— 1 Kings 18:46

One small spark can quickly turn into a consuming fire. With the right amount of heat, starting a fire is actually quite easy. Keeping that fire going, however, is an entirely different matter. To ensure any fire stays ablaze, we need more than just heat; we also need a steady supply of fuel and oxygen. We may experience a spark of passion for God here and there, but we need more than that to keep our fire going for the long run.

So how do we get the spiritual fuel and oxygen we need to keep living for Jesus? How do we build the endurance to consistently live passionately for God? How do we prevent the frustration that comes when our fire keeps going out? I believe the answers to these questions are found in Hebrews. It is here that our life for Christ is compared to a race, and we are offered four ways to build up the endurance to keep running and burning for Jesus. We are instructed to do so by (1) fixing our eyes on Jesus, (2) running the race marked out for us, (3) throwing off everything that hinders us, and (4) running with perseverance. (Hebrews 12:1-3)

These are four lessons Elijah is about to quickly learn. He asked for it and got the fire, but now he is about to face the toughest race of his life. It would seem he would be encouraged for quite some time by God's fire on Mount Carmel, but we will soon see that any celebration was short-lived. Trying to keep that fervor and fire for God burning would become his biggest challenge. So let's look at this part of Elijah's life like a race. We will apply each lesson from Hebrews to our journey with Elijah to see what it truly means to not just get the fire, but to keep it ablaze for the long run.

EYES FIXED ON GOD

Now that the Israelites have witnessed the truth and power of God for themselves, it was time for the drought to stop. So Elijah approaches King Ahab and makes an interesting prediction about the weather. He tells Ahab:

> *"Go, eat and drink, for there is the sound of a heavy rain."*
> *– 1 Kings 18:41*

Weather predictions are usually based on two factors: what happened previously and what is currently happening.[12] Elijah, however, predicts that rain will come even though there has not been a single drop of dew in the last three and a half years, and there are currently no clouds in the sky. Elijah is not making his prediction based on the past or the current weather. He is basing his prediction on who God is, apart from the past or current conditions. We can look back and see God has faithfully provided for Elijah. God has heard Elijah's prayers and protected his life over and over again. Based on his past, Elijah knew God would also fulfill His promise to allow it to rain again at Elijah's word. (1 Kings 17:1) So if God said it, then a heavy rain was coming no matter the situation.

This provides a powerful lesson about the kingdom of God. If our pasts were a reflection of our futures, the forecast would be grim and hopeless, would it not? But our futures are what God says they will be. All who choose Jesus Christ have hope, joy, peace, and true love to look forward to. The blessing is that we can look forward to all the fullness of knowing Christ despite what we've done in the past or even what has been done to us. Our past might have been cloudy. It might have even been catastrophic. But in Christ, our future looks bright. **In the kingdom of God we are not our pasts; we are His daughters.**

> IN THE KINGDOM OF GOD WE ARE NOT OUR PASTS; WE ARE HIS DAUGHTERS

Elijah has clear vision of what is to come, so he knows how to respond. He is not looking to the past or even the present. He is focused on God. God is truly his guide. So if we are to endure and withstand the tests and trials that come with a life dedicated to Christ, we must keep our eyes focused on Him alone. We must not allow our actions and decisions to be determined by our past or present, but who God has been to us all along.

Elijah understood this. Without a cloud in sight he predicted not just any rain, but a heavy rain—an abundance of rain. As we learned from the consuming fire last chapter, God is in the business of going above and beyond our expectations. (Ephesians 3:20) So Elijah tells Ahab to go up from the valley they are in, and to eat and drink. What a relief that must have been to Ahab. They had gone all day waiting for Baal to answer with fire, only to receive no response. It had been a long and draining day, but it was now almost over, and the drought would soon be over as well. Unlike Ahab, however, Elijah does not go up to eat and drink, but to pray.

Although the rain would only come back at Elijah's word, he knew his word was nothing without God's power. So in Elijah-like fashion, he humbles himself before the Lord and prays. He then sends his servant to go and look toward the sea to check for any signs of rain, but there were none. Six times Elijah prays, sends his servant, and receives word that there is no sign of rain. So Elijah keeps praying. That's what we do when we are in a situation out of our control. We pray to the One who is in control. We learn from Elijah that our fire for God starts with prayer, and it is by that same prayer that we keep our fire burning. The Bible tells us to "pray without ceasing." (1 Thessalonians 5:17 ESV) So I love how Elijah did not forget about God after his prayer for fire was answered. Just because God grants us a request does not mean we stop praying. Prayer is how we keep our focus on God and how we prevent ourselves from being distracted by the world. Prayer reminds us where our help comes from, and it reminds us why we are running and burning for God in the first place.

So Elijah keeps praying and sending his servant to see if his prayer has been answered. On the seventh time, Elijah's servant brings back word that there is a cloud the size of a man's hand rising from the sea. That is all the sign Elijah needs. He knew where that small cloud came from and that much more was to follow. So he sends warning to Ahab to stop eating, load his chariot, and head back to Jezreel so he will not be stopped by the rain.

Then the sky grew black, the wind rose, and a heavy rain began to fall. Now that the Israelites had repented and acknowledged the LORD is God, God was not stingy in blessing them with rain. He was ready to pour out a blessing they could not contain. It's like God had been just as anxious to give them rain as they desired it, but like any good parent, He was not about to reward bad behavior. I wonder what we might be missing out on due to our disobedience. I wonder what blessings God is holding back while waiting for us to repent and turn to Him. Look at the Israelites. Once they turned back to God, God was not hesitant to open the floodgates.

So now that God had answered Elijah, it was time

to go back to Jezreel. But I want you to notice that Elijah was not about to leave until God answered his prayer. He was not about to start his journey without God. I'm reminded of Moses' words to God as he prepared to lead the Israelites into the Promised Land:

> *"If your Presence does not go with us, do not send us up from here. How will anyone know that you are pleased with me and with your people unless you go with us? What else will distinguish me and your people from all the other people on the face of the earth?" – Exodus 33:15-16*

Moses was not willing to go anywhere without the presence of God. The Promised Land—filled with milk and honey, and a place he would find rest—was not worth a journey without God by his side. Moses was not focused on the end destination; his eyes were focused on God. Let us not get ahead of God by trying to rush to the finish without Him. **This race is not about the results as much as it is about God.** It is His presence that gives our running and burning purpose, making it all worth it. May our eyes be fixed on God, and may we resolve not to go anywhere without Him.

THIS RACE IS NOT ABOUT THE RESULTS AS MUCH AS IT IS ABOUT GOD

RUN THE RACE MARKED OUT FOR YOU

The biggest challenge to keeping our eyes on Christ will be the temptation to look at how others are running their race. With social media we can know exactly how the lives of both friends and strangers are going. We can now see what type of car they drive, where they went to school, or if they breast or bottle feed. We know what they had for breakfast, lunch, and dinner, how they apply their makeup, and if it's date night or not. But looking at them will not fuel us to run the specific race God has for us. This would be a lesson Elijah needed to understand on his journey from Mount Carmel back to Ahab's palace in Jezreel.

While Elijah was praying for rain, Ahab enjoyed a meal. Ahab then had a head start back to Jezreel as Elijah left after him. Ahab rode his chariot while Elijah went by foot. If the journey from Mount Carmel to Jezreel were a competition, we would say it was unfair. And it was. The evil King Ahab had the best conditions to get ahead. But this did not distract Elijah. Remember, Elijah was focused on God, not his competition. Elijah knew that to finish the race, he must stay in his lane. He must run the race marked out for him and not the one marked out for Ahab.

In our walk with God it is so easy to become

distracted by those running beside us. We look at what they are doing, how they are doing it, and how ahead of us they are. Then feelings of discouragement, discontentment, and envy weigh us down as the gap between us and them seems to grow. It's even worse when the people we are looking at do not serve God or even respect Him, yet seem to be doing better than us. However, we must realize that comparing our race to that of others is a trap to get us off track. We only get distracted by looking at the Ahabs in our lives who seem to have more than us. We are then tempted to think that serving God is not all it's cracked up to be, and our fire for Him starts to fade. We start looking to our sides, and we lose sight of our purpose and mission. Even more, we forget that our strength does not come from having things,

> **OUR STRENGTH COMES FROM A GOD WHOSE POWER CAN TAKE OVER IN OUR LIVES AT ANY MOMENT TO FULFILL THE PURPOSES HE HAS FOR US**

looking a certain way, or knowing influential people. **Our strength comes from a God whose power can take over in our lives at any moment to fulfill the purposes He has for us.** So Elijah does not need a meal right now, or a fair start, or even a chariot. The Bible tells us:

The power of the LORD came on Elijah and, tucking his cloak into his belt, he ran ahead of Ahab all the way to Jezreel. – 1 Kings 18:46

Ahab had the power of men. Elijah had the power of God, and that was all he needed. With God's power Elijah miraculously makes a thirteen-mile journey on foot, arriving in Jezreel before Ahab.[13] The lesson here is simple: God's power can take us further than man's. Whatever God has for us, He will empower us to do it no matter how many odds are against us. Jesus encourages us:

"With man this is impossible, but with God all things are possible." – Matthew 19:26

Key words: with God! God is the One who has prepared the journey specifically *marked out for us,* and no one else. So how someone else finishes her race is not always how God will empower you to finish yours. Your focus should not be on others, but on the One who called you to the race in the first place. Our job is like Elijah's: keep our eyes on God and stay in our lane.

THROW OFF EVERYTHING THAT HINDERS

Elijah was focused on God. He had waited on God to answer his prayer for rain, and he received the very power of God. But his arrival to Jezreel would present some serious stumbling blocks. Once Queen Jezebel finds out about what happened on Mount Carmel, she becomes furious and sends a messenger to Elijah to tell him that within the next day she will have him killed. But I wonder, if Jezebel was so enraged at Elijah and so set on his death, why not send an assassin instead of a messenger? We can make many speculations as to why she did not have him killed immediately, but ultimately we know she did not have the authority to do so. Elijah was in God's hands and he was off limits. The enemy can only do to us what God allows. Even the enemy had to get permission from God before he could bring numerous tests and hardships to Job. (Job 1:12; Job 2:6) Elijah was in God's will and out of Jezebel's jurisdiction. So all she had the power to do was send a threat—an empty threat at that because not only would Jezebel never kill Elijah, but Elijah never died. He was taken up to Heaven in a whirlwind. (2 Kings 2:11)

So Jezebel's threat that Elijah would die was more than ambitious. It was a flat-out lie. But Jezebel did not need to tell the truth if she could simply get in Elijah's head. And that is exactly what she did. Her threat, although as false as her gods, completely got Elijah off his mental game. Like in any race, sometimes the toughest part is not the physical battle but the mental battle. It's the pressing through the thoughts that pop in our head as we run the race marked out for us: *You're not doing enough. This won't make a difference. It's crazy to think you can actually reach that goal. You're wasting your time. God does not care that much. It's really not that serious; you're doing too much.*

These are the thoughts that weigh us down and make our race harder than it needs to be. But if we keep going despite those negative thoughts, those mental weights make us stronger. Because when we finish through the mental challenge, those thoughts are exposed for what they really are: lies, all lies. This is why we must be careful about who we are listening to, and we must be ready to throw off any lies that contradict the truth of our God. Most runners listen to upbeat music because it encourages them to push harder and go further. In the same way, what we listen to has the power to affect our walk with God. If we are going to finish this race for God and continue to burn for Him, we need to make sure we are allowing God's truth and not the lies of this world to influence us. The truth is this: God is enough, this race is worth it, God loves you more than you know, and you *can* run this race with Christ. The Bible encourages us:

> *I can do all this through him who gives me strength.*
> *– Philippians 4:13*

God will give us strength for this race just like He did for Elijah. But lies will slow us down if we keep listening to them, and they will stop us if we believe them. Elijah was caught off guard by his welcome back to Jezreel. He should have been greeted with respect and thanksgiving for starting to bridge the gap between the Israelites and their God. Instead, he is met with death threats. He is hated for his service to God. We too may face this same hate and scorn because we live for Christ.

The good we do may be ignored. Our compassion may be met with hate, and our love with scorn. But we do not run for the world. We run for God. And the world hates that. A war may be raged against us for our devotion to God, but it will not prevail. Jezebel formed the weapon, but it would not prosper. She could send a messenger, but she could not send an assassin. The life of Elijah was out of her jurisdiction, and the only thing she could hit him with was a threat and a lie. But, oh, how the enemy knows that sometimes that's all he needs. Just one *You look fat today; you're a bad mom; no one respects you at work; your church friends don't think you're good enough; you really think God forgave you of that?* can ruin your whole day, week, or even life. The enemy knows he does not have to physically touch us to affect us. He knows that the whisper of even the smallest lie, if not thrown off, can send us spiraling out of control and get us completely off track. And that is exactly what happens to Elijah.

RUN WITH PERSEVERANCE

Elijah becomes fearful of Jezebel's threat and runs for his life. Elijah expected the fire at Mount Carmel to spark a national revival to turn the Israelites from Baal back to God alone. However, he is faced with death threats and King Ahab who is still allowing Jezebel to call all the shots. After all Elijah has been through—confronting Ahab, patiently waiting by the ravine, being tested while in Zarephath with the widow and her son, and seeing God answer by a consuming fire—it's just too much to think that things might remain the same. It's too much to think that all of his faith and obedience have been in vain. Things are not going as expected, and Elijah has had enough. He travels in the wilderness for one day, sits under a bush, and then says to the Lord:

"I have had enough, LORD," he said. "Take my life; I am no better than my ancestors." – 1 Kings 19:4

Since Elijah focuses on Jezebel's lie and not his God, he finds himself in a place of depression, fear, and guilt. He doesn't simply want to quit and walk away from his calling; he wants to end his very life. He does not feel worthy to run this race and live for God. He's had enough and can't take it anymore. If he does not die now he is sure this race will kill him. This is where believing the lies of this world will take us. If you've found yourself in a dark place, I urge you to pray to God to cover you in His truth. Pray He exposes each and every lie over your life with the truth of His Word. Maybe you were told you are worthless. Maybe you were told you will never amount to anything. Maybe you were told you are never enough. Maybe you were told that all the bad in your life is all your fault. I rebuke those lies in the name of Jesus Christ. You are a daughter of the King. You have purpose and destiny, and we need you running this race. We need your life, your testimony, and your fire.

After praying for the rain to stop, praying for the widow's son to live, praying for fire, and then praying for the return of rain, Elijah now says another prayer–he prays for death. He prays the Lord will take his life. And after all those answered prayers, God does not answer this one. **Unanswered prayers are sometimes our biggest blessings.** Maybe you've been praying for something and God has answered, "No." That "no" may very well be your protection, your safety, and your well-being. God wants the best for us, and if He knows we desire something that is not good for us, He will graciously deny our request. But although God denies Elijah's request, He still responds to his need. Elijah falls asleep under the bush and is then touched by an angel who tells him to get up and eat. Elijah finds some bread and water near him, and he eats, drinks, and then falls back asleep.

God's response to Elijah has many spiritual implications about how God is our daily bread and our living water, and how spiritually we need Him to fill us up daily. But I want to address how God actually meets Elijah's physical needs. God knows Elijah is completely fatigued from all that has taken place. So He miraculously provides bread and water. This is an important reminder that God cares just as much about our physical needs as our spiritual needs. He knows that both are important because in this world we need both to survive. I love that Psalm 23 tells us:

He makes me lie down in green pastures. He leads me beside still waters. He restores my soul. — *Psalm 23:2-3 ESV*

Many times we need to allow God to lead us to physical rest so He can then grant us spiritual restoration. There have been many times in my life where I felt off and just not myself. There have been times where I felt down, discouraged, and acted out of character. And most of those times it's because I was simply tired. I just needed to take time to rest and replenish. God is not expecting us to be super women. We do not get extra points for running on fumes. God understands we need food and rest just as much as prayer and quiet time with Him. God wants us to take care of our bodies and treat them like the

MANY TIMES WE NEED TO ALLOW GOD TO LEAD US TO PHYSICAL REST SO HE CAN THEN GRANT US SPIRITUAL RESTORATION

Holy Spirit-dwelling temples that they are. (1 Corinthians 6:19-20) We need rest and to pace ourselves if we are to maintain the endurance we need to finish our race well. God knew Elijah needed to be replenished physically so much so that He sent a second serving of bread and water to Elijah. Then the angel said to him:

"Get up and eat, for the journey is too much for you."
—1 Kings 19:7

The journey is too much for us. We are not crazy, we are not weak, and we are not less-than if we feel it's all too much. If we feel we can't keep up with the demands of life and just never have enough, we are not wrong to feel this way because it's true. This journey *is* too much for us. There's just no getting around that fact. So when we stop pretending that it's not too much, when we stop believing the lie that perfection here on earth can be obtained, when we stop seeing our weaknesses as a lack of our worth, then we can set aside the weights of guilt, shame, and fear, and start going farther than we have ever gone.

After being strengthened by the much-needed food and rest, Elijah travels forty days and nights until he reaches Horeb, known as the mountain of God. On his own, Elijah traveled one day in the wilderness before he prayed for death under that bush. Just one day. But with God, he travels forty days and nights. We can't win this race alone. We can't keep our fire burning without the necessary fuel it needs. The journey is too much for us. It's time we run with the power of God resting upon us, because we can go much further and burn much longer with God than without Him.

REFLECTION QUESTIONS

1) Many times when we find ourselves off course in life it's because we have lost focus. In your walk with God, are you focused on God or something else? Are there any distractions in your life that may be leading you off course?

2) Comparison and looking at others is a sure way to hinder our boldly walking in God's purpose for our lives. Have you found yourself comparing your race to anyone else's? How do you think your walk with God is unique?

3) When life becomes challenging we all face times, like Elijah, when we just want to give up. If you are ready to throw in the towel, ask yourself, *Am I operating in fear or faith? Have I invited God in this journey with me, or am I trying to do everything on my own?*

PRAYER

Dear Heavenly Father, thank You for walking with me on this journey of life. I am never alone with You by my side. I pray for the endurance and focus to keep my eye on the prize: You. I love You. In Jesus Christ's name I pray. Amen.

CHAPTER NINE

Burn Out: How to Persevere When You Want to Quit

The LORD said, "Go out and stand on the mountain in the presence of the LORD, for the LORD is about to pass by."
— 1 Kings 19:11

My most embarrassing moment occurred while running track in high school. I ran a little bit of everything: long distance, short distance, and even some field events. But my most challenging race was the 300 meter hurdles. This is an almost quarter-of-a-mile race *with hurdles*. I never wanted to run that race, but my coach put me in it because no one else would do it. The first time I ran the 300 meter hurdles was the most embarrassing moment of my life. I did fine the first 200 meters of the race, but as I came around the curve of the track to finish off that final 100 meters I felt my body completely shut down. It was just too much, and in my exhaustion I tripped over a hurdle. I stumbled to regain my balance, but then I completely fell down to the ground as I tried to jump over the next hurdle. Everything went in slow motion after that. I saw the other runners zooming by me, and I could hear the gasps from the crowd. I was completely embarrassed and could not wait to get off that track to never run again. I was so frustrated because had those hurdles not been there, a 300 meter run would have been a walk in the park. But that's not how races go, do they? In the same way, our walk with God is not always going to be easy. Sometimes we will face hurdles and obstacles that will make us want to quit the race never to return.

If you remember, we did not leave Elijah on a good note last chapter. He faced some of those hurdles and obstacles, and he was ready to quit. Depressed and discouraged, Elijah had run from Jezreel and prayed that God would take his life. So God replenished him physically with food and rest, but now it was time for Elijah's soul to be restored. God's consuming fire at Mount Carmel was not enough. Elijah needed Mount Horeb where he would encounter the very presence of

God. We don't simply need to see the miracles, blessings, and the work of God. Sometimes not even those things are enough. We need to see God Himself. **We don't only need a picture of what God is like; we need His very presence in our lives.** And God's actual presence is the cure Elijah receives for the spiritual depression we left him in last chapter. It would serve as the encouragement Elijah would need to get through this dark time, dust himself off, and keep going.

WE DON'T ONLY NEED A PICTURE OF WHAT GOD IS LIKE; WE NEED HIS VERY PRESENCE IN OUR LIVES

OUT OF POSITION

We know God has been speaking to Elijah, but now on Mount Horeb we have the rare opportunity to get some popcorn, pull up a chair, and actually listen in on their conversation. While Elijah is in a cave in the mountain, God starts off with a question:

"What are you doing here, Elijah?" – 1 Kings 19:9

What *is* Elijah doing here? God had previously caused His power to fall on Elijah that he might run from Mount Carmel all the way to Jezreel on foot and arrive even before King Ahab who had a head start on chariot. Surely God had not enabled Elijah to do all that simply for Elijah to run out of town. Surely God had not provided for Elijah just for him to call it quits. Surely God had not prepared Elijah to run from his calling. There was a time for hiding by the ravine and with the widow of Zarephath, but now was not that time. The season for hiding was over, and Elijah's usefulness to the Lord would now be found in the public eye. But you would not find him there, and God justly asks why.

I'm reminded of Adam and Eve in the Garden of Eden. God told them not to eat from the tree in the middle of the Garden. When they did and realized their sin, they hid from God. And just like God asked Elijah, He asked Adam, *"Where are you?"* (Genesis 3:8-9) God is all-knowing, so there is nothing going on that He does not know about. God knew where Adam was, but His question served to get Adam to think about it. Adam's answer would cause him to come to terms with the fact that he was not where he was supposed to be. He was not where God had called him to be, or else God would not have asked this question in the first place. Adam and Eve were out of position because they chose to do their will over God's. And now they were ashamed and hiding in the Garden that God gave them dominion over, and were faced to think about God's question: "Where are you?"

Does that question make you nervous? If God were to ask you where you are, would you be in a position of hiding in shame, running from your calling, or far from His will? Would you be like a deer in headlights, or like a child caught with her hand in the cookie jar? I wonder if God's question took Elijah by surprise. I wonder if his mind scrambled for an answer. Nevertheless, Elijah responds:

> *"I have been very zealous for the LORD God Almighty. The Israelites have rejected your covenant, torn down your altars, and put your prophets to death with the sword. I am the only one left, and now they are trying to kill me too."*
> *— 1 Kings 19:10*

Elijah has a lot to say. He responds to God's question with many reasons for being out of position. He answers God first by defending himself and explaining that he has been very zealous for the Lord. This is true. He has been faithful and obedient, but something has changed in Elijah's heart. The man who once interceded on behalf of the Israelites at Mount Carmel so they might know God, now becomes their accuser. Instead of serving the Israelites, he is now comparing himself to them. He has been zealous, but they have not. He gives God a list of all they have done wrong: they rejected God's covenant, tore down God's altars, and killed off the prophets of God. But Elijah's last sentence reveals the major concern of his heart. He tells the Lord, "I am the only one left, and now they are trying to kill me too." Elijah is essentially saying, "I've been faithful, they have not, and if they succeed in killing me, who will serve You, Lord? Who will carry out Your plan? So I've taken matters into my own hands, and I've run away because if I die, then how will Israel turn back to You?" This is Elijah's excuse for being out of position. He doesn't believe things are going according to plan. This is why he "ran for his life." (1 Kings 19:3) and is not in Jezreel. But now that Elijah has given his reasons, it is time for God to respond with an answer that will help Elijah quickly get back into position.

FACE TO FACE

If you have ever been in a long-distance relationship you know how much of a challenge distance can be on the communication that every relationship desperately needs. Donald and I dated for over three years before we were married, and for about a year of that time we were long distance. I was in North Carolina finishing school, and he was working in Washington, D.C. Even with all the technology available to keep in touch daily, it was still a challenging season. There is just nothing quite the same as actually being in someone's presence—seeing his facial expressions, clearly hearing the inflections in his voice, and picking up on all the nonverbal communication cues you miss by simply talking on the phone, texting, or sending an email.

One time in particular during our season of long distance things got really difficult. Our communication was off, and we were having challenges getting on the same page. So one day while I was at a ministry event, I looked over my shoulder and who did I see? Donald. He came to surprise me. Just being in each other's presence was a relief. Even more, it was just what we needed to reconnect and get back on track.

So before God responds to Elijah, He calls him closer. He tells Elijah to come out of the cave he is in and to stand on the mountain. God wanted to ensure that no distance between Him and Elijah would prevent Elijah from clearly hearing what He had to say. God wanted to avoid any miscommunication that might keep Elijah off track and off focus. So before they continue, God prepares Elijah for His presence because He is about to pass by. This conversation will be face to face. I just love how gracious God is to help Elijah. I love how He does not brush Elijah off or turn His back on Elijah. In His patience, God takes time to pause, stop, and actually be with Elijah.

I cannot stress the importance of taking a pause with God, and the value of quality time with Him. Does it take time out of our already busy schedules? Yes. But is it an absolute necessity for our spiritual well-being? You better believe it! This time together was God's primary answer to Elijah's spiritual unrest. And it is also the answer to ours. Maybe you've found yourself at a dead end with no solution in sight like Elijah. You are frustrated, anxious, and scared. Our first response should not be to figure out all the details, but to find peace in God. It is then that we can gain the calm and clarity we need to move forward. Our peace does not come from completed projects, a spotless home, accolades from man, or trying to solve all the world's problems. Our hope does not come from perfect relationships, a flawless appearance, or a huge salary. **God does not need everything in our lives to be perfect in order to give us peace, hope, and clarity. He just needs us to be still enough to be in His presence with a heart ready to listen.**

Our wedding counselor asked Donald and I what is the most important thing a marriage needs. In unison we answered, "God." Wrong! He quickly corrected us and said the most important thing a marriage needs is communication. It's the only way to know we are on the same page, or even know we are talking about the same God. Communication in any relationship is of utmost importance to the success of the relationship, and that is especially true for our relationship with God. And when I say communicate I don't mean our only listing off our requests. I mean being sure we also make space to listen to God. Because God is not going to compete for our ear. It's up to us to position ourselves to hear from Him. It's up to us to look for God through the distractions, to un-rush and be still. It's up to us to endure and wait until we hear from God.

WHEN GOD SPEAKS

When God's presence passed by Elijah on the mountain, the earth went crazy. There was a powerful wind, mountains tearing apart, an earthquake, and even fire. The very creation that God made could not contain all His glory without going out of control. The Bible stresses that although God's presence may have caused these natural catastrophes, His presence was not in them. We are told:

> *Then a great and powerful wind tore the mountains apart and shattered the rocks before the* LORD, *but the* LORD *was not in the wind. After the wind there was an earthquake, but the* LORD *was not in the earthquake. After the earthquake came a fire, but the* LORD *was not in the fire.* – *1 King 19:11-12*

Sometimes the closer we get to God, the crazier life becomes, the more challenges we face, and the more persecution we encounter. But what glory awaits those who endure! When life starts to shake us we may be tempted to get on the phone to get advice from our girlfriends, read every self-help book we can get our hands on, or Google an answer. However, when we seek things and people, no matter how good they may be, over seeking God we forfeit an opportunity of receiving an answer from Him directly. I believe Elijah held on to this truth because through the mountain-splitting wind, the quaking earth, and the fire, Elijah did not run away. Even in the midst of the chaos and disaster, he was not about to leave without an encounter with his God. So Elijah waits through the storm, and his waiting is not in vain. The Bible tells us that after the fire, God came to Elijah in "a gentle whisper." (1 Kings 19:12)

We all want this great, transforming, and life-altering experience with God to make us the women He has called us to be. But it's not always a quick, one-step process. Many times it's making choices every single day to hear from God. Maybe you've been choosing busyness, impatience, and seeking other things over choosing to be with God and hear from Him. The good news is that we get to make this decision every day, even every moment. We can decide right now to position ourselves to hear from God. And the even-better news is we do not need a women's conference, a week-long church revival, or an online Bible study. Those things are great, and God certainly uses them all the time to speak to His daughters. But He also speaks to us at the kitchen sink, playing blocks on the floor with our toddler, on our commute to work, or lying in bed at night. **We may very well find God in the most unexpected and mundane places. Like Elijah, we may find Him in a gentle whisper.**

I know this personally. It was a whisper of God that completely changed me. During a very challenging season while in college, I prayed fervently to God every day after work. I would not stop until I felt a little better and started to feel my attitude and heart about the situation change. But one day I clearly heard God speak back to me. It was just what I needed to lift the burden of my difficult situation. There was no church, no pastor, no choir, no shouting, no laying on of hands, no holy water or oil. It was just me and the voice of God. And it was enough.

With all of this talk about hearing from God you might be wondering *How do we know God is speaking to us?* We know God is speaking to us because we know His voice in the first place. And we know His voice by knowing Him. I can't give you a formula on how God will personally speak to you. He might lead you to a Scripture, give you a dream, or it might be a nudging in your spirit. Speaking may not be the best word to use because you may be listening for an audible voice when God communicates in many ways, but the important part is that we get the message. And we won't get it if we're not expecting it, if we're looking in the wrong places, and especially if we do not know God.

When I call Donald I don't ever say, "Hello, this is Christina." Even without caller ID he knows it's me because he knows my voice. He knows my voice because he's been listening to it for the past ten years. We know God is speaking to us when we have developed a relationship with Him that involves spending time with Him and choosing Him daily. The question is not, "Is God speaking?" We know He is. The better question is,

"Do we know the Speaker, and are we listening?"

Good thing for Elijah, he knew God. Through all we've seen Elijah and God go through together we can confidently conclude they had a deep and sincere relationship. So at the whisper of God, Elijah reverenced himself. He covers his face and bows down to his Lord, recognizing this is not just some thought that popped up in his head. He's heard this voice before, so he knew he was in the presence of God. So now that God has Elijah's full attention, He asks again, "What are you doing here Elijah?" Elijah's answer does not change. He holds true to his previous response and feelings. He reverenced God, but the matter was still unresolved. Elijah is consistent in his concerns for his unrewarded zeal for God, the stubborn Israelites, and feeling all alone. But now, face to face, God responds to all of Elijah's concerns.

WHEN GOD ANSWERS

Elijah's first concern is about his zeal for God. Elijah had faithfully served God throughout his entire journey without question. There is no doubting this. So what does God say about all this zeal? He tells Elijah, "Go back the way you came." (1 Kings 19:15) God encourages Elijah to keep doing what he's doing. Keep being faithful, and keep being zealous. Things may not be working out as Elijah planned, but that is no excuse to stop doing what God has called him to do.

God was not about to let Elijah off the hook. From chapter one of this book we learned that Elijah was a servant of God, and nothing was about to change that. Elijah would keep serving even when things did not make sense because a servant is concerned about the affairs of his master, not his own personal plans. We cannot effectively serve God if we're ready to quit every time we don't understand a matter. We are to go back the way we came. Go back to the faithfulness and service we fervently gave to God when things were less challenging because although things may not make sense, we can always trust that God knows what He's doing.

Elijah's second concern was about the Israelites' unfaithfulness. God reached out to the Israelites at Mount Carmel that they might know Him and return to Him. One small problem—they had rejected the covenant God wanted to reestablish with them. To this concern, God tells Elijah to anoint the future kings of Israel. God has a plan to ensure the worship of Baal and the killing of His prophets will stop. God was not finished at Mount Carmel; that was just the beginning. God was devoted to pursuing His chosen people, and He would provide the leadership they desperately needed to turn them back to Himself.

The last and seemingly most desperate of Elijah's concerns was his being alone. If he is the last faithful servant of the Lord and he dies, what will happen to the Israelites? What will happen to God's plan for His chosen people? So God tells Elijah to anoint Elisha as his successor. Elijah was not always going to be around to ensure the Israelites continually kept their covenant with God. So God would raise up another prophet to fill the role to which God had called Elijah and continue the mission He had for His people. God's plans were not limited to the life of Elijah, but beyond Elijah. God's plan included Elijah, but it

> **GOD'S PLANS OFTEN INCLUDE US BUT THEY ARE NOT ALL ABOUT US**

was not all about Elijah. **God's plans often include us, but they are not all about us. With or without us, the purposes of God will be fulfilled.**

Elijah was not the only person included in God's plan to reconcile the Israelites back to Himself. While Elijah was giving up in the wilderness, God had already prepared Elisha to succeed him and also reserved an additional 7,000 people in Israel who had not worshipped Baal. I want to point out that this remnant of 7,000 faithful servants of God were in Israel and faced the same persecution as Elijah. Elijah was not alone in his fervent service to God. While he was serving God, God was raising up the next generation of Israelites to carry on. And who knows? Maybe Elijah's service to God had encouraged those 7,000 people. Elijah had no idea how his ministry had impacted these Israelites. It is a lesson to us that we never know how God is using us. We never know who is depending on us to run well. There are people watching us right now who need the encouragement of seeing us finish strong. But they never will if we give up.

GETTING BACK UP

Remember that most embarrassing race I was telling you about? The one where I fell? I wanted to give up. It would have been so easy to just walk off the side of the track and just be done with it. I was exhausted, embarrassed, and I had acquired a cut on my leg right above my knee which I still have a scar from to this day. No one would have judged me for walking off. But I could see the finish line. So I limped my way through and slowly climbed over each hurdle, one leg at a time. Finally, I walked across the finish line. I was beyond last place. The other runners were not even on the track anymore. At this point I was just in the way. I did not receive a trophy, ribbon, or certificate. I was not met with any pats on the back, cheers, or applause. But I did my job, and I finished that race.

What was then my most embarrassing moment is now one that I'm actually proud of. It's a moment I will tell my daughter and son to teach them that getting knocked down does not mean you have to stay down. Just because you are not the fastest, or most praised, or have the most resources and connections, does not mean you quit. Just because you make mistakes or mess up does not mean you stop running. **Wanting to quit does not mean we have to because if God is not finished, then neither are we.**

And after hearing from God, Elijah realized that God was not finished with him. We are not sure if God's response was what Elijah was expecting or even hoping for, but I think he got the point. After God speaks, Elijah does not say another word. God's word was enough, and Elijah complies and goes on to do exactly what God told him to do. After a quick reality check from God, Elijah

IF GOD IS NOT FINISHED THEN NEITHER ARE WE

is now back on track. God gives Elijah just what he needed: His presence to help Elijah take his attention off of himself, and place it where it always belonged—on God.

Sometimes we need the reality check that comes from being in the presence of God to remind us this battle is not ours, but God's. Like Elijah, sometimes we are so close to the battle we forget what we are fighting for, and we want to quit. **It is then that God pulls us close to Himself, whispers to us, and reminds us that we are not fighting for ourselves, and we are not fighting for Him, but He is fighting for us.**

REFLECTION QUESTIONS

1) Elijah was concerned about everything but God. It was this loss of focus that placed him out of the position God had called him to. Are you focused on God or your problems? What can you do today to regain focus and get back on track?

2) The time Elijah spends with God on Mount Horeb helps him to gain the clarity and strength to pick himself back up and carry on with his mission. How and when do you take time to be still and hear from God?

PRAYER

Dear Heavenly Father, thank You for speaking to me. I pray for grace to stay focused on You and to position myself to hear from You. It's all about You, and I trust that. I love You. In Jesus Christ's name I pray. Amen.

CHAPTER TEN

Lit: Living to the Fullest

Then he set out to follow Elijah and became his servant.
–1 Kings 19:21

What a journey this has been! Thank you for taking this adventure of faith with Elijah and me. From Elijah's bold confrontation with King Ahab, to his depression at Mount Horeb; from hiding by the ravine, to God's consuming fire at Mount Carmel; from the widow of Zarephath, to Obadiah; we've come a long way. We've learned some great lessons from the life of Elijah, and we've learned more about the character of our God. We know what it looks like and what it takes to live a passionate life for Christ. But you will have wasted your time reading this book if you finish it and think that all these lessons we've learned only sound like good ideas. I hope by now you see that we are all called to allow God's passion for us to ignite our fire for Him. And this is a call we cannot ignore. Jesus tells us:

> *"Here I am! I stand at the door and knock. If anyone hears my voice and opens the door, I will come in and eat with that person, and they with me." — Revelation 3:20*

Do you ever experience that empty feeling that something is missing in your life? Are you dissatisfied with the things of this world no matter how pleasurable they may be? Do you feel you need more in life, but can't quite figure out what it is? Are you frustrated with the lack of strength, power, and focus you need to be the woman you have been called to be? There is a solution to all these questions. His name is Jesus Christ. He has already decided He wants you. He has already decided He wants to give you peace, satisfaction, and wholeness. Jesus wants to consume our lives. He wants to free us from sin, fill us with joy, grant us victory over our fears, and light our fire to live passionate and purposeful lives. There's just one thing. You need to accept Him into your life.

ANSWERING THE CALL

Since the invention of caller ID we've become accustomed to knowing who is calling us, and we've made the habit of choosing which calls to accept and which ones to ignore. This is good. We do not need to accept every call or every opportunity that presents itself. **Not every person deserves our attention, nor every task our dedication. But Jesus does.** He's proven Himself worthy. He died on the cross in our place that we might know God. Who are we to leave Him waiting outside? Who are we to leave Him hanging? Who are we to ignore Him and act like we're not home? So why is Jesus calling and knocking? What does He want? He tells us:

> **NOT EVERY PERSON DESERVES OUR ATTENTION, NOR EVERY TASK OUR DEDICATION. BUT JESUS DOES**

"I have come that they may have life, and have it to the full." – John 10:10

Jesus wants to give us something that no one else can. He wants us to realize He is the answer we never knew we needed. So before you close this book, I want to look at

one more person who answered the call of God with joy–
someone I hope will spur you on to answer Jesus with an
expectant and faithful "Yes."

In continuing with his mission, Elijah is ordered by
God to ordain the next kings of Israel along with his
successor who would be Israel's next prophet: Elisha.
Elijah's first order of business would be to secure Israel's
spiritual well-being by finding Elisha and confirming his
call to ministry. We will see that Elisha makes important
decisions that I believe we can learn from to confidently
answer God's call on our lives.

Elijah finds Elisha working hard, plowing with
twelve pair of oxen. We can conclude from this
information that Elisha is well-off financially. But he is not
using his wealth as an excuse to be lazy. Maybe this is why
God found Elisha worthy of the call to succeed Elijah.
God knew Elisha would say yes and was ready to work. So
Elijah went up to Elisha and placed his cloak around him.
This cloak was a special garment that signified Elijah as a
prophet of God.[14] Placing the cloak around Elisha was an
invitation for him to follow in Elijah's steps. Once the
cloak is on Elisha, Elijah walks off to carry out the other
instructions he received on Mount Hebron. He was
refocused and on mission.

So now Elisha has to decide if he will be on

mission too. Will he continue in his work, or will he follow Elijah? I want to ask you that same question. After reading this book, are you going to continue in your work, your ways, and your desires? Or are you going to follow Christ? Will you allow Him to lead in every area of your life? Will you respond to Jesus by opening your heart and letting Him into your everyday life?

NO PLAN B

Elisha decided he would accept the call, but there was one important thing he decided to do first. He would confirm his call into ministry by leaving everything else behind. He slaughtered his oxen and burned his plowing equipment. He cooked the oxen meat with the burning equipment and gave it to his people. He completely rid himself of his current work. His thinking was not, *I'll follow Elijah until I get uncomfortable, then I can always go back to plan B.* Elisha was so serious, he completely rid himself of any safety net. He was all in.

Many times we make halfhearted commitments, but God is looking for daughters who are all in. He is knocking with every intention of completing every area of our lives. If we accept Christ with the intention of going back to our old ways once things get difficult, then we have not completely decided to follow Him. If we have an option readily available for us to turn from God when things get hard, I guarantee we will. Our best bet is to completely rid ourselves of people and things that we know we will run to when we feel that following Jesus is

WE CAN GIVE UP OUR BACKUP PLAN TO ANSWER THE CALL

too hard. And after witnessing Elijah's depression in the wilderness, we know at times it does get hard. One of Elijah's saving graces, however, was that he had nowhere to run but to God. Elisha places himself in the same position. Now, there is one last decision Elisha makes in answering his call that is of utmost importance, one that many of us often overlook.

LIVING TO THE FULLEST

After Elisha accepts God's call on his life, the Bible tells us:

> *Then he set out to follow Elijah and became his servant.*
> *– 1 Kings 19:21*

Elisha made the decision to serve. His intention was not to make himself great, but to be a servant. It takes a person with a servant's heart to still pursue the work of God when it costs him. Realizing we are here to serve God will save us a lot of time and frustration. So Elisha gladly humbles himself to the role of servant if it means answering the call of his God. And he does so joyfully, not out of obligation.

Elisha would be a prophet, he would succeed Elijah, and he would do even greater wonders than Elijah, (2 Kings 2:9-15) but he would start off as a servant. Are you ready to see what God wants to do through you for His glory? Are you ready to partner with God and experience His will on earth as it is in Heaven? (Matthew 6:10) Then you must be ready to serve.

If all this talk about service is sounding familiar it's because we've come full circle in our journey. The first thing Elijah told Ahab about himself, even before his name, was that he was a servant of the Lord. And now Elisha is taking this same posture. What do you think God is demonstrating to us here? He wants us to be like His Son, Jesus Christ, who was God in the flesh but took on the role of a servant. The Bible tells us that Jesus "being in very nature God, did not consider equality with God something to be used to his own advantage." (Philippians 2:6)

If Jesus served; if He humbled Himself and came

to earth as a fragile human; if He washed His disciples' feet, and then took on a punishment that we deserved; is it too much for God to ask us to take a similar position? Is it too much for us to live beyond ourselves and think of others and their needs? Is it too much to turn the other cheek, or say we're sorry first, or not defend our positions, all for the sake of glorifying the One who humbled Himself on our behalf?

Pride is one of our worst enemies. It tricks us into thinking it's all about us. It tempts us into believing our sins really aren't that bad, and that we really don't need God that much. It causes us to think our needs and wants are more important than others'. It causes us to live lives run by selfishness, fear, and insecurity. And that is such a waste of a life. But there is a cure for the wasted life: Jesus Christ. As we've already learned, Jesus does not just offer us any life, but a full life.

Sure, we can keep living for ourselves, we can ignore God's call, and we can increasingly partake in the pleasures of this world. We can hide when it becomes hard to be a Christian, or assimilate when our faith gets us in trouble. But that's all we can do. Jesus, on the other hand, offers a life greater than this world, a life full of peace and purpose. Like Elisha, we can give up our backup plan to answer the call. And when we do, I want you to know we will never come away empty-handed. We will have life, and we will have it at its fullest.

So we have some decisions to make. Will we follow God? Will we be all in? Will we serve? These are not easy decisions. But high callings never are. I pray you say, "Yes." I pray you open the door. I pray your passions are for Christ. Will you be perfect? No. Will it be worth it? Yes. Serving Christ is the best decision you can make. It's a decision that will open your eyes to the flames of God's passion for you, flames that will incinerate any desire we have that is not of God. We will only be left to wonder how we ever went as long as we did without choosing Christ. I leave you with one last Scripture:

> *Not that I have already obtained all this, or have already arrived at my goal, but I press on to take hold of that for which Christ Jesus took hold of me. Brothers and sisters, I do not consider myself yet to have taken hold of it. But one thing I do: Forgetting what is behind and straining toward what is ahead, I press on toward the goal to win the prize for which God has called me heavenward in Christ Jesus.*
> *– Philippians 3:12-14*

Keep going, keep pressing, and always burn for Him.

REFLECTION QUESTIONS

1) Looks like we have a decision to make. God is calling us to be His Daughters of Fire by reflecting His glory into a dark world. How have you answered this call? If you haven't, what is stopping you?

2) Elisha was completely committed to following the call on his life, so much so that he rid himself of his plowing equipment because he never planned on going back. Do you have any backup plans that might tempt you when serving God becomes a challenge?

3) Both Elijah and Elisha accepted the role of servant. They did great things in the name of the Lord because they realized this mission was not about them. Jesus, though God, set this same example by living a life to serve us so that we might have salvation. Are you ready to serve and follow the example of Jesus? What are some ways you can serve in your home, church, and community to be the light you are called to be?

PRAYER

Dear Heavenly Father, thank You for the testimony of Elijah. I pray that my life will continually reflect Your love for me as I decide to answer the call to serve You as a Daughter of Fire. I love You. In Jesus Christ's name I pray. Amen.

An Invitation

True fulfillment and purpose can be achieved through a personal relationship with God. Our sin however, prevents us from having that relationship. Since God is holy He cannot allow sin to go unpunished and the result of our sin leads to death. So God sent His only Son, Jesus Christ, to die in our place. Yes, He really loves us that much. That is why we are called His Beloved. Now instead of death, anyone who places their faith in Jesus Christ as Lord of their life and Savior from their sins will be saved. No matter where you are, what you have done, or what has been done to you, God loves you and desires to be in relationship with you. I invite you to begin a relationship with Jesus Christ by praying this simple prayer:

Lord Jesus Christ, I am sorry for the things I have done wrong in my life. I ask for your forgiveness and now turn from everything which I know is wrong. Thank you for dying on the cross for me to set me free from my sins. Please come into my life and fill me with your Holy Spirit and be with me forever. Thank you Lord Jesus. Amen.

About Beloved Women

Beloved Women, Inc. is a 501(c)3 non-profit that encourages, uplifts, and equips women in the love of Jesus Christ and the truth of God's Word. Our vision to see women live in the knowledge of who they are in Christ: His Beloved. Our mission is to provide Bible study resources and community that will encourage and grow women worldwide in a relationship with Jesus Christ. Learn more and join us at **www.belovedwomen.org**

CHAPTER 1 – Stars: Shining Bright in the Dark
[1] Swindoll , Charles. Elijah: A Man Who Stood with God. Nashville, TN: Thomas Nelson2000.
[2] "Night Vision." Wikipedia. 2016. https://en.wikipedia.org/wiki/Night_vision.

CHAPTER 2 – Extinguished: The Quickest Way to Put Out Fire
[3] Barker, Kenneth L, ed. In NIV Study Bible, 499. Grand Rapids, MI: Zondervan2002.
[4] Guzik, D. "Study Guide for John 4 by David Guzik." Blue Letter Bible. Last Modified 7 Jul, 2006.
https://www.blueletterbible.org//Comm/guzik_david/StudyGuide_Jhn/Jhn_4.cfm
[5] "What Does It Mean to Worship the Lord in Spirit and Truth?" Got Questions Ministries n.d. http://www.gotquestions.org/worship-spirit-truth.html.

CHAPTER 3 – Burn: Allowing Any Season to Refine You For God's Best
[6] "How To Refine Gold." Gold Traders Precious Metal Dealers n.d. http://www.goldtraders.co.uk/gold-information/how-to-refine-gold.asp.
[7] Guzik, D. "Study Guide for 1 Kings 17 by David Guzik." Blue Letter Bible. Last Modified 7 Jul, 2006.
https://www.blueletterbible.org//Comm/guzik_david/StudyGuide_1Ki/1Ki_17.cfm

CHAPTER 4 – Fire: Making it Through Tests and Trials of All Kinds
[8] "Commentary on 1 Kings 17 by Matthew Henry." Blue Letter Bible. Accessed 20 Jul, 2016. https://www.blueletterbible.org///Comm/mhc/1Ki/1Ki_017.cfm

CHAPTER 6 – Flicker: Turning Your Wavering Passion For God Into An All-Consuming Fire
[9] "H6452 - pacach – Strong's Hebrew Lexicon (KJV)." Blue Letter Bible. Accessed 21 Jul, 2016.
https://www.blueletterbible.org//lang/lexicon/lexicon.cfm?Strongs=H6452&t=KJV
[10] "Who Was Baal?" Got Questions Ministries n.d. http://www.gotquestions.org/who-Baal.html.
[11] Specific rituals concerning Old Testament sacrifices can be found in Leviticus Chapters 1-7.

CHAPTER 8 – Ablaze: Keeping Your Fire Burning For the Long Run
[12] Muller, Grace. "How Do Meteorologists at AccuWeather Make Your Forecast?" AccuWeather, Inc. 2013. http://www.accuweather.com/en/weather-news/how-do-meteorologists-make-forecast/4716627.
[13] Swindoll , Charles. Elijah: A Man Who Stood with God. Nashville, TN: Thomas Nelson2000.

CHAPTER 10 – Lit: Living to the Fullest
[14] Guzik, D. "Study Guide for 1 Kings 19 by David Guzik." Blue Letter Bible. Last Modified 7 Jul, 2006.
https://www.blueletterbible.org//Comm/guzik_david/StudyGuide_1Ki/1Ki_19.cfm